# THE

# FORECLOSURE FIX!

*12 Proven Steps to Beat the Bank, Escape Foreclosure, and Turn Your Property into a Profitable Asset*

DJ OLOJO

www.theforeclosurefix.com

ISBN: 979-8-9890803-0-4 (paperback)
ISBN: 979-8-9890803-1-1 (ebook)
ISBN: 979-8-9890803-2-8 (hardcover)
ISBN: 979-8-9890803-3-5 (audiobook)

Library of Congress Control Number: 2023922183

Printed in Atlanta, Georgia

Ordering Information:
Special discounts are available on quantity purchases by corporations, associations, and others. For details, contact help@theforeclosurefix.com

Publisher's Cataloging-in-Publication Data
Names: Olojo, DJ (Ayodeji), 1985- .
Title: The foreclosure fix! 12 proven steps to beat the bank, escape foreclosure, and turn your property into a profitable asset / DJ Olojo.
Description: Atlanta, GA : Crepe Myrtle Publishing, 2024. | Includes 30 b&w charts and diagrams.
Identifiers: LCCN 2023922183 | ISBN 9798989080328 (hardcover) | ISBN 9798989080304 (pbk.) | ISBN 9798989080311 (ebook) | ISBN 9798989080335 (audio)
Subjects: LCSH: Foreclosure – United States – Popular works. | Real property – United States – Popular works. | Mortgage loans – United States. | BISAC: BUSINESS & ECONOMICS / Real Estate / Mortgages. | LAW / Real Estate. | LAW / Bankruptcy & Insolvency.
Classification: LCC KF697.F6 O46 2024 | DDC 346.7304--dc23
LC record available at https://lccn.loc.gov/2023922183

# DISCLAIMERS

This book is not a legal guide to handling the foreclosure process. Foreclosure is a serious legal matter governed by the courts and laws of your specific state. If you plan to fight a foreclosure action, it is important that you seek legal counsel to help you. No book can replace the advice of a licensed and experienced legal professional who understands all the details of your specific situation.

This book is not exhaustive and all-inclusive. Real estate, foreclosure, finance, and law are topics that can be discussed ad nauseam. No book can explain all these things in totality. This book is meant to provide you with a cross section of my specific learnings, experiences, and recommendations based on the situations I have encountered in my real estate career. This is not legal or financial advice.

# DEDICATION

This book is dedicated to those stuck in a difficult foreclosure situation who don't know what to do. I pray that this book equips you with the tools to take the next steps toward a better future.

Special thanks to LaShayna, Dad, Mom, Charlie B, Momma B, and the thousands of others who have invested in me. I hope this book will serve as a down payment on my immense debt of gratitude and appreciation.

To all the homeowners—now friends—I have encountered over the years, thank you for allowing me to use my gifts and for teaching me that caring about the person I am trying to help is more important than the real estate I hope to transact. The lessons you have taught me are the catalyst for this book.

# PRAYER FOR THE READER

Heavenly Father,

Please give the reader of this book the wisdom to know what to do in their situation and the courage to do it. Please remind them that they are loved immensely and that this difficult season will pass. Regardless of what happened in their life, let them know that You are for them and not against them and that better things are coming their way. Restore their confidence. Renew their hope. Bless and keep them, shine Your face upon them, be gracious to them, and give them peace. Amen.

# CONTENTS


Introduction......................................................................... 1

Note to the Reader.............................................................. 5

How to Use This Book......................................................... 7

Chapter 1    Reinvent Your Mindset......................................11

Chapter 2    Become Seasonally Selfish............................... 21

Chapter 3    Understand the Bank's Lingo & Motivation........ 29

Chapter 4    Evaluate Your Financial Position......................51

Chapter 5    Identify Your Property Condition & Value.......... 57

Chapter 6    Recognize You Are a Fat, Juicy Target ................ 77

Chapter 7    Make a Decision: Keep the House or Let It Go?.. 87

Chapter 8    Attempt to Keep Your Home .............................. 99

Chapter 9    Know Thy Self and Thy Potential Buyers............121

Chapter 10  Pick Your Preferred Profit Strategy..................... 129

Chapter 11  Master the Sales Process...................................151

Chapter 12  Expect the Best but Prepare for the Worst ..........179

What's Next......................................................................187

Free Foreclosure Resources.................................................191

Glossary ..........................................................................193

Acknowledgments ............................................................199

About the Author.............................................................. 201

Endnotes.......................................................................... 203

# INTRODUCTION

It was a muggy Atlanta day in the dead of summer, and the pollen count was high. Georgia pollen has a not-so-subtle way of reminding you it's there, and a yellow haze coated sidewalks, streets, and vehicles. Even my allergy pills were not enough to stop my eyes from itching and my nose from running. It was the first Tuesday of the month, and although I did not know it then, first Tuesdays like these would become a reoccurring event in my life. Like diehard fans don't miss games, I would never miss a monthly foreclosure auction.

This was my first foreclosure auction experience, and I went as a spectator to witness what it was like. I did not have any money to purchase anything, and I did not know any of the bidders apart from the buddy of mine who had invited me to attend. I did not have a list of properties; I had no clue what was going on. We were on the steps of the Fulton County Courthouse in Atlanta, Georgia. The courthouse looked like it had been built in the early 1900s and had a large stone design on all four sides. A grand staircase provided access to three large metal double doors. The handrails were broad and regal with a crocodile color that had patinated from years in the elements.

On a normal day at the courthouse, people would come and go freely without much ruckus. But auction days are different. The once-cleared steps were filled with investors and spectators of all races and ages, each vying for the opportunity to walk away with one or multiple properties. Often, the crowd would extend to the street and block access into the building. On numerous occasions throughout the day, a deputy sheriff would come outside and yell, "Don't block the walkway. No standing on the steps." This would create a path for the traffic to flow as investors scattered like roaches with the lights turned on, just to return 15 minutes later when the deputy withdrew inside the building.

I always envisioned the auction to be similar to the auctions I saw on TV and in the movies. Some auctioneer with a southern accent and quick tongue would call the property and start the bidding, the bid would fly up, and the auctioneer would create drama and suspense by holding the bid out to the final second before yelling, "SOLD!" This was very different.

An unassuming attorney or representative of a law firm or title agency would come out to the courthouse between 10 a.m. and 4 p.m. on the day of the foreclosure sale and cry a property. The representative often spoke in a normal voice and would not yell out but instead would calmly say, "My name is John Doe, with the law firm of Smith and Jones Legal Group, LLP, and we are crying the property located at 123 Hopeful Street, Atlanta, Georgia, 30312."[1] By the time the representative finished their introduction, numerous investors would surround them and ask them to repeat the property address, the borrower name, or the firm they were with. This would go on for a few minutes before the representative would start to read the legal description and foreclosure notice.

After a few minutes of reading, the representative would say, "The opening bid amount is $152,422, and do I have any bids?"

Bidding would then ensue, or if no one was interested, the property would go back to the bank. This process went on for hours with law firm after law firm, completing hundreds of foreclosure sales.

One particular property sale impacted me in a unique way. There was a family at the auction going around asking investors not to buy their house. It was an African American family, and the father was frantically looking for the attorney with their property. His wife stayed at the bottom of the steps, pushing a baby in a stroller back and forth while asking people if they knew what attorney had her property. They obviously had not been to the auction before because they did not understand how the process worked. Their desperation had led them to attempt one last option: begging strangers not to bid on their home.

I was saddened, annoyed, mad, and perplexed—all at the same time. This led me to ask the question, what had gone wrong?

Was the attorney at fault for doing their job, or was it the callous investor for buying the house to make a profit? Was the homeowner at fault for not paying their mortgage, or was it the lender for giving them a loan they could not afford?

I never saw that family again, but they left an indelible mark on me. Foreclosures are more than just real estate. People are on the other side of the transactions, and their lives are disrupted.

Unfortunately, that day would not be the last time I saw families begging for their homes. I wrote this book with all those desperate families in mind. I was uninformed and unable to help that family on that day, but the last decade of my life has prepared me to give you the solution I could not give them. Enshrined on the pages of this book is your Foreclosure Fix!

# NOTE TO THE READER

I wrote this book because I *care about you!* One of my early real estate mentors always impressed upon me that a real estate transaction is less of a business deal and more of an interaction between two human beings trying to solve a problem. The need to care about the people regardless of the situation has always been my motivation. This book is an expression of care for all those dealing with foreclosure or the prospect of losing their homes.

In my work as a Realtor, licensed builder, landlord, and distressed debt investor, I have encountered numerous quagmires in real estate transitions. I started in the 2009 timeframe, when folks were running from real estate and the headlines of the day were about the housing bubble, foreclosures, and NINJA (no income, no job, no assets) loans. This was my reality as a broke and inexperienced wannabe investor. Investment real estate was like a plague; you were considered lucky if you did not have it as part of your investment portfolio. The real estate bubble had popped, and everyone who was overleveraged was licking their wounds and trying to rebuild.

In the beginning, I primarily purchased foreclosure properties from the county foreclosure auction with one of my college friends/business partners. At that time, it was not uncommon for one county in Georgia to have hundreds of houses going to the foreclosure sale every month. Some houses were sold for as cheap as $1,000. However, as times have changed and market conditions have improved significantly, the homeowner is in a stronger equity position. You now look like a genius if you own real estate.

As foreclosures have slowed down and the market has moved from a buyer's market to a seller's market, it perplexes me that I still see homeowners who are facing foreclosure losing tens of thousands of dollars of equity. At first it was difficult to understand why someone would not make sure they had a roof over their head. I had a hard time synthesizing some homeowners' disconnect between the reality and the fairy tale they believed in their heads. Then I started talking to and dealing with homeowners directly.

Over the years, I have talked with thousands of homeowners facing foreclosure and other difficult situations. I have heard the same complaints, frustrations, and rants. I have cried with and prayed for people. I have laughed with them and been the punching bag for those who are at their wits' end. I have successfully strategized with people, and I have had my time wasted by dubious homeowners. I have witnessed and celebrated the successes of proactive homeowners who took action to change their situations. And, unfortunately, I have watched the failures of those who delayed or ignored the warning signs.

This book is a compilation of all those conversations and experiences. I have seen that those who turn foreclosure into a beneficial and sometimes profitable experience have certain traits and actions in common—and those who roll over and play dead, waiting for the inevitable, have certain commonalities as well. The 12-step plan I've outlined in this book is the secret to fixing your foreclosure problem and turning pain into profit.

# HOW TO USE THIS BOOK

This book focuses primarily on mortgage and deed of trust foreclosures. I do not discuss tax sales or homeowners' association foreclosures. While some of the information about the subject matters is similar, each one is nuanced.

This guide is meant to help you decide on the best next step to take in your situation. I lay out options you can consider and ultimately act on to improve your future. Do not be swayed into thinking that if you do nothing, the problem of foreclosure will mysteriously go away. It will not go away—it will only get worse.

There is a lender to whom you owe money, and they deserve to get paid because you signed a contract. Although things may have changed in your life, that does not negate the contract you signed. Therefore, you must hold up your end of the agreement or attempt to amend the contract.

I do not sugarcoat the truth in this book. If you do nothing, you'll lose your house and potentially suffer financial damage. Fixing a foreclosure situation will take work, time, and energy.

I am an advocate for the homeowner. That means I want *you* to make the best decision for *you!* I don't care if that decision involves a real estate broker, an investor, an attorney, a lender, or anyone at all. I care that you are in a better situation after reading this book.

The majority of the strategies I compiled in this book are not original and were not created by me. The United States residential mortgage industry is an $18 trillion industry.[2] Suffice it to say, many intelligent people are working to address this issue in numerous ways. A quick Google search will allow you to find out what to do if you are in foreclosure. However, just as a good athlete needs a coach to achieve their desired results, you need a coach to help you navigate this situation. Navigating the foreclosure process is convoluted, difficult, stressful, annoying, and complicated. In this book, I will coach you through this situation and give you the 12-step game plan to pick the right plays at the right time.

There are times when it is important to have a narrow focus, and this is one of those times; you need to be obsessive and dogmatic about your goal. This is the fourth quarter, the clock is winding down, your team needs points, and you are the *only* one who can win the game. Everything is on your shoulders. It is your job to execute the plays. I am cheering you on from the sidelines, but your talents and abilities will make you victorious.

My 12-step strategy will set you up for success by allowing you to decide the best plan for your situation. Following the method entirely, not just one or two steps, will provide the best possible financial and emotional outcome. You want to explore the full range of options at your disposal.

## The 12-Step Foreclosure Fix Plan

1.  Reinvent Your Mindset

2.  Become Seasonally Selfish

3.  Understand the Bank's Lingo & Motivation

4.  Evaluate Your Financial Position

5.  Identify Your Property Condition & Value

6.  Recognize You Are a Fat, Juicy Target

7.  Make a Decision: Keep the House or Let It Go?

8.  Attempt to Keep Your Home

9.  Know Thy Self and Thy Potential Buyers

10. Pick Your Preferred Profit Strategy

11. Master the Sales Process

12. Expect the Best but Prepare for the Worst

If you want to keep your house, Chapter 8 will be most essential for you. If your goal is to profit by selling your home, Chapter 9 will be most important because it gives you the secrets that real estate professionals and investors don't want you to know.

## What This Book Is and What This Book Is Not

I am not an attorney or certified public accountant. I do not go over the specific laws of each state. I have provided helpful resources at www.theforeclosurefix.com. I work with attorneys and law firms who practice all over the United States. Laws are constantly changing, so it's best to check for any updates or consult with an expert if you have specific legal questions.

If you are in the small minority of people trying to game the system and get over, this book is not for you. Put it down right now because you will be disappointed. This book is for those who never imagined they would be in this situation. It's for those who have been set back by financial hardships, divorce, death, disease, or the trials and tribulations of life—those who find themselves stuck.

By the end of this book, you will be able to figure out your best-case scenario, worst-case scenarios, and various alternatives, and you will be confident as you proceed.

At the end of each chapter, there is a summary recapping the highlights of the chapter. For free resources to help you or to connect with the Foreclosure Fix community, visit our website at www.theforeclosurefix.com.

CHAPTER 1

# REINVENT YOUR MINDSET

*Knowing ignorance is strength;*
*ignoring knowledge is sickness.*
*— Lao Tzu*

Borrowers in foreclosure experience a wide range of emotions. Some are worried and anxious and scared for the future. Others are checked out and don't care what happens next. Regardless of where you are on the spectrum of emotions, it is important to understand how your emotions play into your decision-making process.

Behavioral neuroscience has shown us that individuals tend to make riskier decisions in response to stress.[3] When a person's emotions are out of control, they tend to make illogical decisions that lead to worse outcomes. I want to help you avoid major mistakes in the challenging foreclosure process. However, before we can address the specific tactics and strategies to deal with your foreclosure problem, we need to make sure you are in the correct state of mind.

From my thousands of conversations throughout my career working with distressed homeowners, there have emerged three simple truths that you need to understand and accept:

1. You are not alone.

2. Foreclosure is a traumatic experience for you and the others impacted.

3. You are responsible for fixing this problem.

## You Are Not Alone

When you google the word "foreclosure," more than 140 million results pop up. That amount of information hints at how common and important this subject matter is. The fact that government agencies, law firms, and businesses are dedicated to this field is further proof of foreclosure's commonality. However, when we are in an emotional state, our knee-jerk reaction is to think that we are alone and the only ones facing financial problems. This could not be further from the truth.

Consider these statistics:

- In 2021, spending on housing made up 16.7% of the U.S. gross domestic product.[4]

- 73% of Americans say money is the number one stressor in their lives.[5]

- Only 51% of Americans and Canadians say they are living comfortably on their present incomes, while 50% and 41% experience negative daily emotions of stress and worry.[6]

- In the first quarter of 2023, 1 in every 1,459 housing units nationwide had a foreclosure filing.[7]

- 324,237 properties in the United States received foreclosure filings in 2022.[8]

- There were 370,685 personal bankruptcy cases filed nationwide in the United states in 2022.[9]

- 63% of Americans live paycheck to paycheck.[10] This means that most Americans—your neighbors, your coworkers, and your friends—are only one bad day away from being in a position similar to your own (or worse).

Don't let Facebook pictures and Instagram Reels deceive you. Many people are struggling; financial woes plague our nation and the world. Life challenges come up for everyone, and unfortunately, things you never anticipated or planned for will happen throughout your life. These tough situations will cause you to have to make difficult decisions.

## Grieving Is Healthy

Foreclosure is a traumatic experience, and it is perfectly expected and acceptable to be upset and mad about your situation. Research has found that a worsened psychological condition and an increase in the prevalence and risk of depression and anxiety emerged as consequences of foreclosures. Foreclosures can also compromise the mental health of others impacted, even if they did not directly experience foreclosure themselves.[11]

No one plans to buy a house and lose it in foreclosure. When you signed hundreds of pages of loan documents while having the euphoric experience of purchasing your home, you weren't doing so with the thought that you would wake up one day and be in a situation where you were receiving legal notices or knocks on the door from the sheriff. Nor do people plan to get sick and be in a situation where they don't have enough income to pay their bills.

Everyone expects and dreams about paying off their homes in full and early—or, better yet, being able to one day buy their dream homes with all cash! We envision the wonderful memories we will make at our homes: the family gatherings, dinner parties, and celebrations. However, when the unexpected happens, it is important to take time to grieve. You have a right to be frustrated, upset, and overwhelmed because this situation is not going the way you planned. You need to address this emotional roller coaster and embrace the grieving process.

The five stages of grief are denial, anger, bargaining, depression, and acceptance.

## Denial

- "This is not happening to me! The bank made an error, and my property is not in foreclosure."

- "I know I have not made my payments and my situation has not changed, but I will get the money somehow, and everything will be okay."

- "This foreclosure will go away if I ignore it."

## Anger

- "Why me? I'm a great person. This should not be happening to me."

- "I'm in this predicament because of someone else."

- You take out your emotions on your family and anyone else who will listen.

- You yell at, curse out, hang up on, or cry with the helpless mortgage servicer call center representatives.

## Bargaining

- You begin to negotiate with yourself about how to get out of the situation. "I'm going to be a better person, start going to church, start helping others."

- "A miracle is going to come and take away this problem."

- "Maybe if I can hold on a few more months, things will get better, and I won't have to do anything."

## Depression

- You feel like you can do nothing to change the situation.

- You ignore the mail, email, calls, texts, stacks of bills, etc.

- You pretend like you are not in foreclosure.

## Acceptance

- You come to terms with what is happening and can now move forward.

- You regain your will to fight.

- You start figuring out a plan.

My goal for you—and the goal of this book—is to help you get to the acceptance stage as quickly as possible. When you get to the acceptance stage, you can take decisive actions that are not clouded by the baggage of your experiences in the other stages. This is the stage where you can work toward the results you want and profit from a lousy situation. This is the headspace you need to be in if you want to make the most out of a bad situation.

For you, foreclosure is very personal, but for everyone else involved, it's just business. You must learn to overcome your emotions and work toward a solution.

My cousin is an emergency room physician. I often ask him to tell me about his craziest emergency room experiences. He has gut-wrenching and tear-jerking stories that are very sad, and often the patients in his stories do not live. I ask how he copes with dealing with so much death. His answer centers around the fact that doing so is part of his job. He gets excited because he saves significantly more people than he loses. He focuses on the good in a difficult situation. You need to do the same thing.

Research has shown that the health benefits from positive thinking include increased life span, greater resistance to illnesses, and greater psychological and physical well-being, just to name a few.[12] You need to focus on the things you can do to bring about the outcome you desire. You now must focus on what you can control, change, and impact.

## You Are Responsible for Fixing This Problem

When you get to the stage of accepting the situation, you will have to take complete ownership.

Let's complete a simple exercise. Say the following words out loud. With every successive statement, get louder and louder.

- This is *my problem to fix.*

- This is *my problem to fix.*

- This is *my problem to fix.*

- This is *my problem to fix.*

- THIS IS MY PROBLEM TO FIX.

- THIS IS MY PROBLEM TO FIX!!!!

Why did I ask you to do that? Reading aloud reduces stress and can improve memory.[13] I want you to remember that THIS IS YOUR PROBLEM TO FIX. You don't have to fix it alone, but you must be the catalyst to move the process along. You are 100% responsible for the outcome.

A few years back, I was conversing with a lady about her house that was scheduled to be sold at foreclosure auction in 30 days. I spoke with this lady multiple times over the 30-day period, and she assured me that she had everything taken care of and was going to file bankruptcy to save her home. I told her on multiple occasions that she should not delay, and I encouraged her to file bankruptcy as soon as possible. Fast-forward to 2 p.m. on the day of the foreclosure auction, and my phone rang. It was the same lady calling me, hysterical and in tears. She was upset and inconsolable because she thought she had filed bankruptcy the day before the sale, but she never received a confirmation, and the bankruptcy court had never received her filing. Unfortunately, she lost her house. In that moment, I wanted to ask her, "Why in God's name did you wait until the day before the sale to do something? You had so much time." I did not ask and just listened. Don't let this be you.

Initially, I was perplexed that people I talked with or attempted to help with their foreclosure situation would wait until the last minute to do something about the problem. They did not take action or make important decisions until a few weeks or even days before the foreclosure sale. However, I have come to understand the impact of avoidance coping, decision inertia, and procrastination due to the stress foreclosure places on the homeowner.

If we ignore the problem, it's not there—or at least, it feels that way temporarily. Avoidance increases anxiety.[14] You have to fight against the feeling that you may have to do nothing. You can't let this situation get the best of you and have you paralyzed or fearful. This is not the time to curl up in the corner and wish it will go away, nor to close your eyes and hope to wake up from this bad dream. It won't go away, and this is not a dream.

If you were not in this situation and you were talking to a friend who was, what would you advise them to do? How would you advise them to act?

You need to fight every urge to procrastinate and wait until tomorrow. There will always be something else to do. You need to make time to fix this problem right now. You can't and won't fix everything at once, but you need to start taking small steps today.

What do small steps look like? Well, I'm happy you asked:

- Reading this book.

- Listening to *The Foreclosure Fix* podcast.

- Asking someone for help.

- Signing up for The Foreclosure Fix newsletter at www.theforeclosurefix.com.

Don't be like the people who I have spoken to over the years who didn't take ownership of their situations and lost their homes.

---

# Chapter Goal & Key Thoughts

## Chapter Goal

The goals of this chapter are to inform you that you are not alone in foreclosure, to give you permission to grieve, and to remind you to take full ownership of this situation.

## Key Thoughts

- There are a myriad of statistics and data that show that a majority of Americans have financial woes and are stressed about money.

- The five stages of grief are denial, anger, bargaining, depression, and acceptance.

- The quicker you can start the grieving process and get to the acceptance stage, the more time you have to plan for the outcome you want to achieve.

- You will need help from others on your foreclosure journey, but you are 100% responsible for the outcome.

### CHAPTER 2

# BECOME SEASONALLY SELFISH

*Nothing resembles selfishness more
closely than self-respect.*
— *George Sand,* Indiana[15]

The word "selfish" has a negative connotation. As kids, we are told to share, and as adults, we are told to be generous. I 100% agree with generosity and extending a helping hand whenever possible. However, there is a time and place for everything.

I have created the term "seasonally selfish." If you are facing foreclosure or are in pre-foreclosure, then now is your time to be seasonally selfish. You should not feel bad about it, and you do not owe anyone an explanation or apology. You have permission to pull back and focus on yourself instead of focusing on everyone else.

Being seasonally selfish means taking time out for a specific season to work on things that are important to you. You block out all the distractions and noise to allow yourself the time needed to focus on yourself, specifically your well-being and current financial situation.

I have listened to countless stories from homeowners who are selfless but on the verge of losing their homes. They bailed their child out of a jam, helped a family member, or invested in a business that someone told them would be the next big thing. They were being kind and helpful to others while being shortsighted and harmful to themselves.

As a property manager, I have seen multiple tenants who have healthy adult children living in the home and struggle to pay the rent while their children go unscathed. In some scenarios, the adult child was unemployed or had inconsistent employment. They got to stay home while the parent tried to find a way to provide. Being benevolent is a good way to live, but *only* when your *house* is in order. Right now, your *house* is in foreclosure, so you need to prioritize yourself.

You see people being seasonally selfish all the time, but you may have never realized it. When an athlete gets injured and they take months away from their sport to rest, heal, and recover, that is being seasonally selfish. When an expectant mother takes maternity leave from work to deliver and care for her new baby, that is being seasonally selfish.

What happens if the athlete or mother does not take the time for themselves? They cause significantly more damage and make the situation worse. Furthermore, neither person is in the state of mind to show up as the best version of themselves while they are dealing with their situation. When they take the time off they require, though, they come back refreshed, rejuvenated, and revived.

## Lose Your Ego

There are tons of emotions and memories connected to a home. We imagine the meals we ate around the dinner table, the smell of Grandma's cooking in the kitchen, the heat of a lit fireplace on a cold winter afternoon, the sounds of children playing in the backyard, and the sizzle of burgers on the grill.

Our homes are a source of pride, and they command respect, whether because we are the first in our family or circle of friends to own a property or because we have built up our reputation in our community as always having it all together. The prospect of our self-esteem and pride being negatively impacted can outweigh the financial hardships we are facing.

What if the perception you are trying to keep up is all in your head, and those who you are trying to impress already know the truth? Maybe it is the roof leak you still have not found time to repair or the broken appliance you can't seem to replace that gives it away. Maybe it's the unkept yard or the gutters that are filled with pine straw and growing plants. Let me tell you a secret: everyone already knows.

Let me remind you, there is no need to seek social approval. Those who really love you don't care about your material possessions. Lose your ego and stop pretending.

Don't let the negative stigma of what others think stop you from doing what you know you need to do. You are not here to impress anyone else. You are here to show up for yourself and show up for your family. You need to do that now more than ever. That might mean selling a car or selling other valuables. It might mean getting an additional or better-paying job. It might mean distancing yourself from friends or stopping communication with certain individuals. Whatever it means in your specific situation, you need to do what you need to do in order to move forward in this season.

Sometimes, the people around you may not like that. Sometimes, you may have to adjust your lifestyle. Sometimes, you may have to resign from the country club or cancel expensive memberships. Sometimes, you may have to give up fancy dinners or disconnect from social media. This is the time to focus and recalibrate your lifestyle.

## You Don't Need to Give a Timeline

I enjoy playing and watching basketball. I had a phenomenal basketball career in elementary and middle school. However, my basketball dreams were crushed in high school when my 5'10" frame stopped growing and I was no longer the best player in my school. Two of my favorite players are LeBron James and the late Kobe Bryant. I love to watch them play and marvel at the shots they make and what their bodies can do. Yet one of the things I found interesting is that before games, especially big games or in key moments or during time-out breaks, seconds before they had to take big shots, you would see them alone for a moment. Maybe they were in the locker room with their headphones on, sitting on the bench in a trance, or on the court talking to themselves. They took moments to focus inward to manifest the results they wanted to see.

You need to do the same. It may be for a few days. It may be for a few weeks. It may be for a few months. Or it may be for the foreseeable future.

You can't do anything for anyone else if you don't have a roof over your head. You need to make your main focus at this point in time saving your house or making money off the sale of your house.

## Worry About Yourself First

In my previous career, I traveled frequently. It was not uncommon for me to be on multiple planes and in multiple cities in the same week. I flew so often that I got to the point where I practically memorized the flight safety briefing announcements. One thing that stuck out to me is how they would always remind us on every flight, "In the case of an emergency, place the breathing device on yourself first, before helping anyone else." There is profound knowledge that you can take away from this. ***In the case of a foreclosure emergency, take care of yourself before taking care of anyone else.*** You are no good to anyone if you are in a bad place financially, mentally, and emotionally.

I was once conversing with a lady named Betty about purchasing her home. Betty had a reverse mortgage going into foreclosure, and she wanted someone to purchase the property. Betty was around 70 years old (I never ask a lady her age), and the property was in disrepair. She rented a room to a 50-year-old mechanic who paid her $100 per week, and in return, he cut the grass and helped her around the house.

Because the loan was a reverse mortgage, Betty did not have any mortgage payments; all she had to do was pay taxes and insurance, but she was not even able to do that.

I asked Betty, "Do you have any children?"

She replied, "Yes, I have a son and a daughter, and they both live less than an hour away."

I asked, "Do they know about the foreclosure?"

Betty said, "Yes, but they are too busy to help me."

I was upset by her comments, but I continued, asking her what her desired outcome for the situation would be. Betty replied, "I want to pay the back taxes and homeowner's insurance so the bank can stop the foreclosure. I'm old and will probably die soon, but I want my kids to have my house."

Betty was about to be homeless and destitute, but she was still worried about the children who were too busy to help her when she needed them the most. *Don't make the same mistake.* We know that homeowners who experience a foreclosure have higher than average levels of anxiety and depression.[16] Don't be so worried about your kids, friends, and family that you forget about yourself. Become seasonally selfish now, and start taking the steps needed to avoid foreclosure.

## What Actions to Take Immediately

So, what does being seasonally selfish look like in action?

Being seasonally selfish is going back to the people you loaned money to and asking them to pay up. Tell them to pawn their stuff, drain their retirement accounts, and give you what is owed.

Being seasonally selfish is asking your kids and family to help you out in this time of crisis. Please note that this does not work if you are the one who people are always bailing out. You cannot be a repeat offender.

Being seasonally selfish is telling your friends that you are not going out to dinner because you must save money and eat in.

Being seasonally selfish is selling the expensive car with a high car note and getting a cheaper car.

Being seasonally selfish is saying *no* to distractions and time wasters and *yes* to yourself!

Being seasonally selfish sounds like saying no to many things and yes to your *house!*

In college, I was in a show choir. I made the choir due to my smooth baritone voice rather than my dancing skills. Our choir practices were a breeze for me, but our dance practices were a completely different story. Although I consider myself an average dancer, I did not particularly enjoy the type of dancing we did in show choir. Our performances were similar to those in a Broadway musical. The problem was that I would sometimes forget the routines, get off beat, or forget to catch my partner. I was more enamored with the singing than the dancing.

Our choreographer was a phenomenal dancer, and she did not take any mess. She was the opposite of patient, and she would make us stay at rehearsal until everyone knew the routine perfectly. She would punish us with grueling exercises when we messed up too many times or when she was frustrated with our effort. She would tell us that the exercises were conditioning and that the calisthenics would help us perform better. I thought that this was a form of cruel punishment and that she was getting back at us for messing up her well-choreographed routines.

Often, when someone (most likely me) messed up the routine and the group was upset with the slacker (me), she would vehemently yell, **"You are not a baby. Get the titty out of your mouth."** This phrase, although mildly graphic, has always provided me with a sense of clarity when I have to make a difficult decision or do something I don't want to do. She was telling us to toughen up, not be lazy, stop whining and crying. Just do what we had to do and move on.

Is it time for you to get the titty out of your mouth?

## Chapter Goal & Key Thoughts

### Chapter Goal

The goal of this chapter is to remind you to take the necessary time to deal with your foreclosure situation.

### Key Thoughts

- Being seasonally selfish allows time to heal and focus.

- The word "NO" is a good and acceptable answer in many situations.

- There is no need to provide a timeline for your process.

- The people who love you don't care about your material possessions.

### CHAPTER 3

# UNDERSTAND THE BANK'S LINGO & MOTIVATION

*Banks are to the economy what the heart
is to the human body. They cycle necessary
capital through the whole, and they are barely
noticed until pressure, necessity, or crises.*
*— Hendrith Smith*

## The Bank Does Not Want Your House

There is an idea in pop culture that your lender wants to own your house. I have heard hundreds of homeowners say, "The bank just wants my house because the property values have increased!" Let me inform you that the bank does not want your house. They can and will take your house, but they don't *want* your house. Either you will pay the debt, or your house will pay the debt.

What the bank really wants is for you to pay them according to the terms of the loan agreement. If you have ever examined a mortgage amortization table—the chart that breaks down the principal and interest in each mortgage payment—you will notice that it is front-loaded with lots of interest. When you make a payment at the beginning of your loan, most of your payment goes toward interest, while only a small portion goes to principal. This is not an accident. This is the math that lenders understand and have created a trillion-dollar industry on.

See the example below of a $300,000 loan at 6% interest over a 30-year term.

| Year | Interest | Principal | Ending Balance |
| --- | --- | --- | --- |
| 1 | $17,899.78 | $3,684.04 | $296,315.96 |
| 2 | $17,672.56 | $3,911.26 | $292,404.71 |
| 3 | $17,431.32 | $4,152.50 | $288,252.21 |
| 4 | $17,175.21 | $4,408.61 | $283,843.60 |
| 5 | $16,903.29 | $4,680.53 | $279,163.07 |
| 6 | $16,614.61 | $4,969.21 | $274,193.86 |
| 7 | $16,308.12 | $5,275.70 | $268,918.16 |
| 8 | $15,982.72 | $5,601.10 | $263,317.06 |
| 9 | $15,637.26 | $5,946.56 | $257,370.50 |
| 10 | $15,270.49 | $6,313.33 | $251,057.17 |
| 11 | $14,881.10 | $6,702.72 | $244,354.45 |
| 12 | $14,467.69 | $7,116.13 | $237,238.32 |
| 13 | $14,028.78 | $7,555.04 | $229,683.28 |
| 14 | $13,562.80 | $8,021.02 | $221,662.27 |
| 15 | $13,068.08 | $8,515.74 | $213,146.53 |

| | | | |
|---:|---:|---:|---:|
| 16 | $12,542.85 | $9,040.97 | $204,105.57 |
| 17 | $11,985.22 | $9,598.59 | $194,506.97 |
| 18 | $11,393.20 | $10,190.61 | $184,316.36 |
| 19 | $10,764.67 | $10,819.15 | $173,497.21 |
| 20 | $10,097.37 | $11,486.45 | $162,010.76 |
| 21 | $9,388.91 | $12,194.91 | $149,815.85 |
| 22 | $8,636.75 | $12,947.06 | $136,868.78 |
| 23 | $7,838.21 | $13,745.61 | $123,123.17 |
| 24 | $6,990.41 | $14,593.41 | $108,529.76 |
| 25 | $6,090.32 | $15,493.50 | $93,036.26 |
| 26 | $5,134.71 | $16,449.11 | $76,587.16 |
| 27 | $4,120.17 | $17,463.65 | $59,123.51 |
| 28 | $3,043.05 | $18,540.77 | $40,582.73 |
| 29 | $1,899.49 | $19,684.32 | $20,898.41 |
| 30 | $685.41 | $20,898.41 | $0.00 |

**Note: Numbers are rounded.**

The average mortgage or deed of trust term is 30 years, but the average mortgage only lasts about 10 years before it is paid off, refinanced, or goes delinquent.[17] (*Note that some states use mortgages, while others use deeds of trust. For the purposes of this book I use "mortgage," but they are interchangeable.*) This means that by the time the average mortgage is paid off, the borrower has paid mostly interest, leaving the bank with a nice profit on the money it loaned out. In the example provided, after 10 years, the borrower would have paid approximately $166,895 in interest and $48,943 in principal payments. Over a 10-year period, the homeowner has paid three times more in interest than they have paid to principal reduction. This is why the bank does not want your house. They want your money!

Houses are complicated and come with liability. They have maintenance issues, mold, lead, yards that need landscaping, things that need servicing, and, most importantly, each one is different. Mortgage notes are simple, and lenders like simple. There is a promise to pay and a security instrument against a piece of property. The math for the loan is spelled out in the document that everyone already signed. It is simple. Bankers like simple things, which is why, again, they don't want your house; they want your money!

Our firm once had to foreclose on a house in Virginia. The property was being used as a rooming house and was in poor condition when we got it back after the foreclosure sale. We immediately had to spend money on attorneys to file for eviction. This process took numerous months before the occupants vacated.

Now that we had possession of the property, we had to send a locksmith to rekey the locks. We had to send a landscaper to cut the grass. We had to send a contractor to inspect the property, take pictures, winterize the pipes, and provide a property condition report. We had to send out a real estate broker to provide us with a broker's price opinion. We had to send out a clean-out crew to trash out the property. We had to get insurance on the property. We had to maintain the property and ensure the condition was safe and sightly while we advertised the property for sale. In short, we had to spend time and money.

After the property had been on the market for a while, we accepted an offer lower than our asking price. The property closed, and we eventually got some of our money back. Yes, I said *some* of our money—after spending a year and a half dealing with attorneys, contractors, real estate agents, and vendors, we had a net loss of over $15,000. We had never wanted the home; we had wanted the borrower to pay us as agreed.

Take the same loan example we used above on the $300,000 house. If the borrower kept this loan to maturity and made on-time payments over a 30-year period, the borrower would have paid $647,515 for the home. This is more than double the original mortgage amount. And, provided that most homeowners don't keep their loans until maturity, the lender stands to make a nice profit. Hopefully you can begin to see why banks don't want to own your home.

## Lenders Come in All Shapes and Sizes

When most people think of mortgage lenders, they think about big banks—Wells Fargo, JPMorgan Chase, Bank of America, etc.—and rightfully so. These companies spend billions of dollars on marketing and real estate so that you think of them first for your banking needs. Large banks are just one of the many kinds of lenders in the mortgage marketplace, though. Lenders vary in size and objectives.

There are also many smaller lenders—credit unions, local banks, insurance companies, pension funds, private companies, family offices, and not-for-profit organizations—that provide home loans. Some of these entities specialize in investor loans, non-conforming loans, loans with higher perceived investment risk, loans for specific industries or asset classes, or loans for underrepresented groups and/or first-time homebuyers.

Some mortgages are seller-financed, meaning that when the buyer purchased the house, the seller provided the loan to the buyer. The seller of the house now becomes the bank, and their loan is secured by the house they just sold. So, in some instances, it is not uncommon for the lender to know the borrower.

The other confusing and frustrating fact is that mortgage loans are purchased and sold all the time. Sometimes, the sale happens shortly after origination, while other times, it happens many years later. The terms of the loan don't change for the borrower, but where they send payments may. The Consumer Financial Protection Bureau requires borrowers be informed when a loan is sold or transferred. You need to be aware that the company who originated your loan might not be the same company that is filing foreclosure. If the lender foreclosing is not the same lender you received the loan from, that does not automatically mean it is a scam.

Put yourself in the shoes of a lender.

Would you give a loan to a stranger and not expect to make a profit? If you said yes, then you are kindhearted, and I admire you.

Would you make thousands of loans to strangers and not make a profit? If you said yes, you are lying or very rich. LOL.

Lenders can't run at a deficit for an extended period of time. Most must make a profit to survive. Lending is a business. Lenders lend money to make money. They take on risk because they know some of their loans will default. To combat delinquency, some government-backed loans charge mortgage insurance to help offset the loans that will inevitably become delinquent.

The details of the securitization of debt and the role government, institutional lenders, hedge funds, and other parties play in our economy is a complex and vast topic that entire books and portions of the government are devoted to. For the purposes of this book, suffice it to say that you should take it seriously if a lender is filing foreclosure on you.

## What Is Foreclosure?

*Merriam-Webster* dictionary defines "foreclosure" as "a legal proceeding that bars or extinguishes a mortgagor's right of redeeming a mortgaged estate."[18]

I define "foreclosure" as the bank saying, "You are going to pay me back my money or I'm taking your house!"

> The foreclosure process differs by state. Some states are judicial, meaning the foreclosure must be conducted by the court system. Other states are nonjudicial, meaning that the foreclosure can be completed without the courts. Some states have a process for both judicial and nonjudicial foreclosures. A map outlining the judicial versus nonjudicial states is below.

## Judicial Foreclosure and Nonjudicial Foreclosure[19]

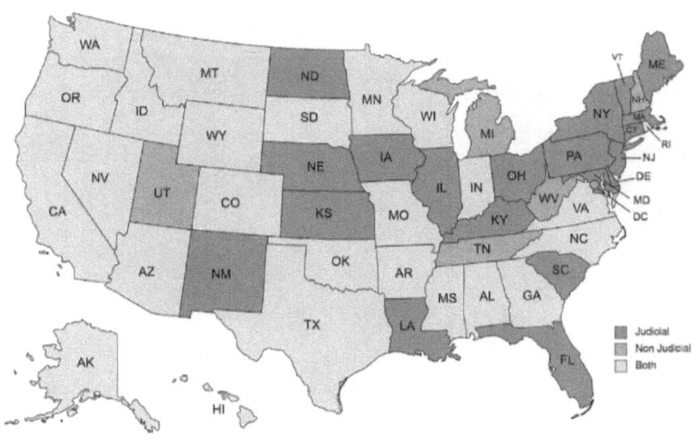

I have also provided a chart of the foreclosure timeline and redemption period by state.[20]

| State | Judicial | Non-Judicial | Foreclosure Timeline | Redemption Period | Deficient Judgement |
|---|---|---|---|---|---|
| Alabama | ✓ | ✓ | 1 - 3 Months | Up to 12 Months | Yes (Judicial) |
| Alaska | ✓ | ✓ | 3 - 4 Months | None | Yes (Judicial) |
| Arizona | ✓ | ✓ | 3 - 4 Months | Up to 6 Months | Yes (Judicial) |
| Arkansas | ✓ | ✓ | 4 - 5 Months | Up to 12 Months | Yes |
| California | ✓ | ✓ | 3 - 5 Months | Not Likely | Yes (Judicial) |
| Colorado | ✓ | ✓ | 2 - 5 Months | None | Yes |
| Connecticut | ✓ | | 5 - 6 Months | Court Determined | Yes |
| Delaware | ✓ | ✓ | 3 - 7 Months | None | Yes |
| District of Columbia | | ✓ | 2 - 4 Months | None | Yes |
| Florida | ✓ | ✓ | 4 - 6 Months | Yes | Yes |
| Georgia | ✓ | ✓ | 2 - 3 Months | None | Yes |
| Hawaii | ✓ | ✓ | 3 - 4 Months | None | Yes |
| Idaho | ✓ | ✓ | 5 - 6 Months | None | Yes |
| Illinois | ✓ | | 7 - 10 Months | Yes 3 - 7 Months | Yes |
| Indiana | ✓ | | 5 - 7 Months | None | Yes |
| Iowa | ✓ | | 5 - 6 Months | 12 Months | Yes |
| Kansas | ✓ | | 3 - 5 Months | Up to 12 Months | Yes |
| Kentucky | ✓ | | 5 - 6 Months | Up to 12 Months | Yes |
| Louisiana | ✓ | | 2 - 6 Months | None | Yes |
| Maine | ✓ | | 6 - 10 Months | 90 Days | Yes |
| Maryland | ✓ | | 2 - 3 Months | Court Determined | Yes |
| Massachusetts | ✓ | | 3 - 4 Months | None | Yes |

| Michigan | | ✓ | 2 - 3 Months | Up to 12 Months | Yes |
|---|---|---|---|---|---|
| Minnesota | ✓ | ✓ | 2 - 3 Months | 6 Months | Yes (Judicial) |
| Mississippi | ✓ | ✓ | 2 - 3 Months | None | Yes |
| Missouri | ✓ | ✓ | 2 - 3 Months | Up to 12 Months | Yes |
| Montana | ✓ | ✓ | 4 - 6 Months | 12 Months | Yes (Judicial) |
| Nebraska | ✓ | ✓ | 5 - 6 Months | None | Yes |
| Nevada | ✓ | ✓ | 3 - 5 Months | None | Yes |
| New Hampshire | | ✓ | 2 - 3 Months | None | Yes |
| New Jersey | ✓ | | 3 - 10 Months | 6 Months | Yes |
| New Mexico | ✓ | | 4 - 6 Months | 9 Months | Yes |
| New York | ✓ | | 4 - 8 Months | None | Yes |
| North Carolina | ✓ | ✓ | 2 - 4 Months | 10 Days | Yes (Judicial) |
| North Dakota | ✓ | | 3 - 5 Months | 60 Days | No |
| Ohio | ✓ | | 5 - 7 Months | Until Confirmation | Yes |
| Oklahoma | ✓ | ✓ | 4 - 7 Months | Until Confirmation | Yes |
| Oregon | ✓ | ✓ | 4 - 6 Months | None | No |
| Pennsylvania | ✓ | ✓ | 3 - 9 Months | None | Yes |
| Rhode Island | ✓ | ✓ | 2 - 3 Months | Up to 3 Years | Yes |
| South Carolina | ✓ | | 4 - 7 Months | None | Yes |
| South Dakota | ✓ | ✓ | 6 - 9 Months | Up to 12 Months | Yes |
| Tennessee | | ✓ | 2 - 3 Months | Up to 2 Years | Yes |
| Texas | ✓ | ✓ | 2 - 3 Months | None | Yes |
| Utah | ✓ | ✓ | 4 - 5 Months | 180 Days | Yes |
| Vermont | ✓ | | 7- 10 Months | Up to 6 Months | Yes |
| Virginia | ✓ | ✓ | 2 - 3 Months | None | Yes |

| Washington | ✓ | ✓ | 4 - 5 Months | None | Yes (Judicial) |
|---|---|---|---|---|---|
| West Virginia | | ✓ | 2 - 3 Months | None | Yes |
| Wisconsin | ✓ | ✓ | 6 - 10 Months | None | Yes |
| Wyoming | ✓ | ✓ | 2 - 3 Months | 3 Months | Yes |

Delinquency/Pre-foreclosure starts when a borrower defaults and misses payments on the loan. The pre-foreclosure process can last numerous months or years depending on the type of loan, type of servicer, judicial or nonjudicial state, or workout options available to the borrower. Active foreclosure begins when the attorney files the civil lawsuit or records the legal documents initiating the process.

Here's what the process typically looks like:

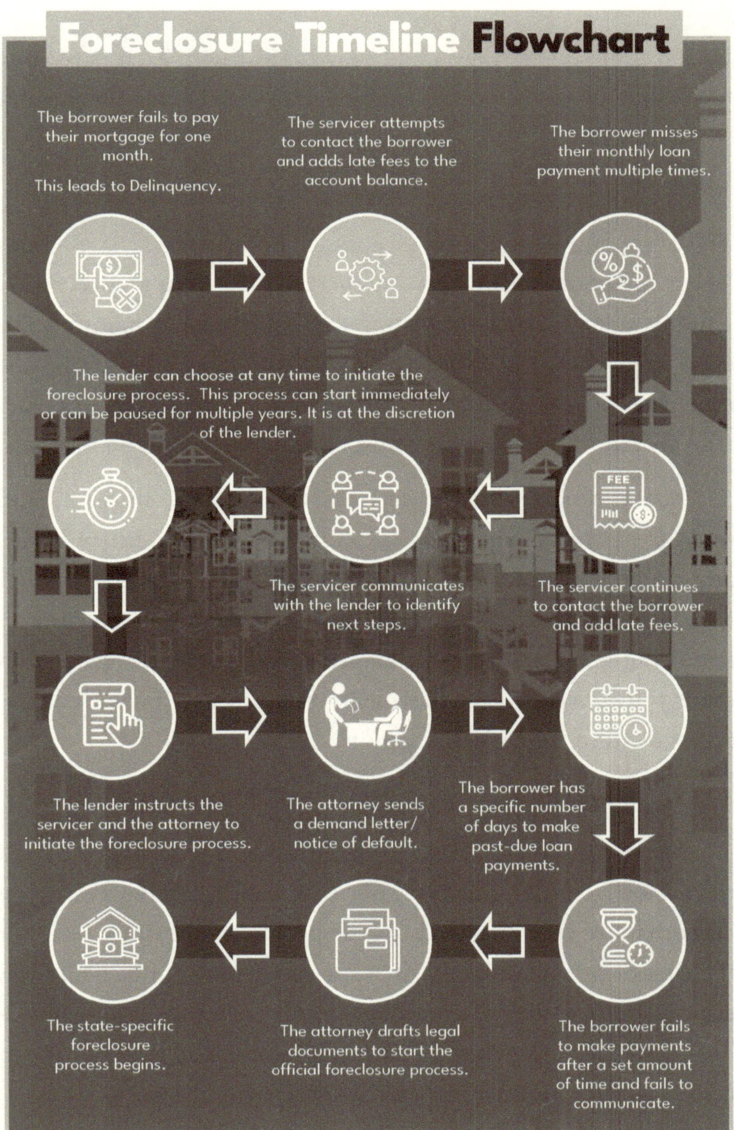

## The Important Parties
## (And How to Deal with Each of Them)

Understanding the players and how to deal with each party in a foreclosure is very helpful to your success in navigating the process.

### Loan Servicers

There are numerous misconceptions homeowners have about lenders. The most common misconception is that the company sending you your statements and calling you every month is the exact same company that owns your loan. This is not always the case. Due to the regulations, insurance, expertise, and licenses required, mortgage notes are most often serviced by loan servicers.

Loans servicers are companies that collect, monitor, and manage mortgage notes for their customers. Banks, hedge funds, and noteholders are their primary customers. The borrower is their secondary customer, and they act on behalf of the bank in managing and tracking your loan file. This is the company who sends you your mortgage statements and provides you with online access to all of your account details.

The simple fact is that some loan servicers are terrible.

Being a mortgage servicer is hard work. Servicers make their money on volume. You typically have hourly employees doing tasks that are very important to the people on the other end, but these tasks are monotonous. These people hear the same issues and excuses daily, so they often become numb to individual situations. This does not mean they are not well-intentioned or won't try to help you, but it means that your sad story will not work.

One area in particular that homeowners take issue with regarding loan servicers is their call centers. Many businesses have bad call centers, but call centers are particularly frustrating with loan servicers because of the importance of the transaction. It can be the most infuriating process to be put on hold and get bounced around from one representative to another. Every time you speak with someone, you are starting over and providing what feels like your whole life story, again and again and again. It is maddening. But it is necessary, and in their defense, the job of a servicer is difficult.

One of the reasons why the process is convoluted and painful is because banks and servicers are not set up to deal with delinquent loans. They have the ability to handle them, but delinquent mortgage loans do not work the same way as delinquent products in other industries. My wife's favorite store is Target. When you purchase something from Target online or in person, the return process is simple. You can call and get a return label, or you can take it to the customer service counter and get your money back. Target wants to make this process as easy as possible for you because they want you to come back and spend more money in their stores or online. Retail stores are used to returns because 16.5% of items are returned every year.[21]

The servicer handling your mortgage does not have the same incentives to provide an optimal customer service experience. First, you are stuck with them and must work with them to resolve the problem. Second, loan servicers have had to downsize, and their loss mitigation departments are not as big as they once were. Your loan file is not a standard file anymore, so you will have to speak with a special department. Last, they have already attempted to reach out to you to rectify the problem, and now that you are reaching out to them, they don't mind if you have to wait. Based on the stats provided in Chapter 1, less than 1% of homeowners are in active foreclosure, so the focus of the loan servicer is on the other 99% of performing loans instead.

When dealing with loan servicers, the name of the game is follow-up. The following are key steps to save yourself a lot of time and aggravation.

1. Open your mail and loan statements.

2. Answer your phone when the servicer calls.

3. Call numerous times when you need to reach the servicer.

4. Call early.

5. Block off time in your schedule to call.

6. Be patient.

7. Get the name, ID number, email, and/or phone number of the person you are talking with.

8. Ask to speak with the manager of the department you are talking to.

9. If you call and get someone who is not helpful, call back. Sometimes you need to get a better or more experienced representative.

10. Request information via email, fax, and mail. You want to get the information the fastest way possible. If you don't know how to use email, ask someone for help.

11. If you call and can't understand the person you are speaking with because of their accent, ask to speak with another representative or call back.

12. Expect to be put on hold for a long time.

13. Ask for an email recapping what you discussed.

14. Have a pen and paper handy when you talk with your servicer and keep good notes of the conversations.

15. Communicate over the phone and in writing via email or mail.

16. Expect to call back multiple times.

17. Expect to be annoyed, agitated, and angry.

18. Expect to have to wait three to seven business days for a payoff or reinstatement quote. The servicer will not give you these numbers over the phone on your first request because they have to calculate all the attorney, legal, and late fees.

19. Expect to overcommunicate. The worst thing to do is to not communicate.

When I say, "Be patient," I mean it. I have spent over four hours dealing with a servicer, trying to get information and details on a loan. I was hung up on multiple times when different representatives attempted to transfer me to someone else. I was put on hold and had to listen to elevator music for 20 minutes at a time. I had to wait while they researched and talked with different colleagues. It was an infuriating process. But, in the end, I was able to get the information I needed.

The lender and servicer typically don't care about what happened to you. Your situation is not emotional for the bank; it is business. Your situation may be sad, your situation may be unfortunate, but they hear lots of unfortunate situations and sad stories. The customer service rep may listen to your story, they may try to empathize with you, but the customer service rep does not make the policies and often does not have the power to change the guidelines of the bank. These are large institutions with multiple layers of people involved, so it is unlikely that you will be successful in having a conversation with someone to sway them in your favor.

## Lender/Bank

This is the company, bank, or person you owe money to. This company owns the mortgage note and has the mortgage or deed of trust on your property. This might not be the same party who originated the loan because loans are often purchased and sold. Some lenders have a policy of selling their non-performing assets because they don't want to have the headline risk of foreclosing on homeowners.

## Dos and Don'ts

**Don't** contact the loan officer who originated your loan, expecting that they know exactly what's going on with your file. Once a loan is created, the loan officer's job is done, with the exception of relationship management for your future financing needs. The newly originated loan now moves on to the servicer.

**Don't** ignore communication from your lender or servicer.

**Don't** think of your lender as your enemy nor your friend.

**Do** think of the lender as your partner. You both made an agreement, and your obligation is to fulfill the commitment you have made to them or to remedy the issue by making an alternative arrangement.

**Do** utilize lender- or government-provided counseling or foreclosure-prevention programs.

**Do** know that the size of the lender and type of loan matters. If you have a large bank or institution, it will most likely be harder to negotiate the terms. If you have a government-backed loan, there are standard policies and guidelines that will be used. If you have a smaller lender, such as an individual, hedge fund or smaller company, you have a greater likelihood of dealing with someone higher up in the food chain. They will still have standard operating procedures as well, but you may get quicker responses and turnaround time. Smaller organizations have fewer layers. If you go into the local pizza shop to buy pizza, you can probably walk in and talk with the owner. However, if you go into a large pizza chain, you can speak with a manager, but you won't get to talk to the president. This is no different.

A few misconceptions people have about mortgage lenders and banks:

1. **Lenders always make money on every loan.** Mortgage holders can and do lose money. Legal fees, property condition issues, real estate broker fees, bankruptcy costs, etc. add up quickly.

2. **Lenders want your house.** Debunked previously.

3. **Lenders will not negotiate.** You have to ask. Some will negotiate and some will not, but you won't know unless you try.

4. **Lenders will go away if you don't respond.** Sometimes, lenders don't want to spend the resources on your loan file. They may have more important issues to deal with. They are patient and may sell your loan to another company that will pursue your matter. Or they will patiently wait. The odds are that if they do nothing, in 10 years or less, a life event will happen that will cause you to deal with them. They are on title and figure that eventually you will come around.

5. **Lenders own your home once you stop paying or leave the property.** Neither your lender nor your servicer owns your property until the foreclosure sale is completed or you sign it over to them. Even if you walk away from your home, most loans will not automatically revert to the lender. The lender can secure the property and maintain their investment if the property is vacated, but they are still not the owner until the foreclosure process is 100% complete. There will be a deed recorded in the county records showing their ownership.

## Foreclosure Attorney

The foreclosure attorney is retained by the lender/servicer to handle the legal aspects of the foreclosure process, court proceedings, and legal advertisements. The foreclosure attorney could be a small one-person firm or a multistate firm with thousands of employees. Depending on the size of the law firm, you may never talk to the attorney on the legal documents you receive. You may talk with a paralegal or someone on the foreclosure team. This is not uncommon, and it doesn't indicate that they have anything against you. Some firms specialize only in this area of the law, so they have teams set up specifically for this.

Foreclosure attorneys, just like servicers, get their fair share of people who are calling to curse them out or provide tear-jerking stories about why they can't or won't pay. I recommend that you save your time and energy. The attorney, while they might care, does not have the power to stop the foreclosure process. They are working on behalf of their client, and their client is the one making the decisions. Now, if you want to pay but need a little more time or have a legitimate plan, the attorney, asset manager, and servicers might be open to hearing what you have to say.

The average timeline to complete a foreclosure as of Q1 of 2023 is around 950 days.[22] However, don't be deceived by this number, thinking time is on your side. The foreclosure timeline varies widely by state. States like Louisiana, Hawaii, and New York can average double this amount of time, while states like Wyoming, Texas, and Arkansas can take a small fraction of the average.

I provide this information to highlight a few things. Some people believe that dragging out the foreclosure process is a smart move. They get to live without paying a mortgage for months or even years. This is not the case. The longer a foreclosure process drags out, the more expensive it gets for all parties involved, especially the homeowner. A significant portion of the legal costs incurred by the lender are recoverable and will be paid by the borrower.

You are paying for your procrastination. When a lender pays an attorney to send you a demand letter, formal legal documents, or any correspondence, they charge that back to you. A law firm that is charging hundreds of dollars per hour for their attorneys is racking up a large bill on your tab. There is a Fannie Mae fee schedule that many attorneys use for their foreclosure services. However, it is not mandatory for all types of litigation, and many attorneys bill their time hourly instead. Also, the fee schedule does not cover everything an attorney might have to do on a foreclosure file.

I recommend thinking twice about dragging out a foreclosure case just for the sake of it. You might not like the bill on the other side of it. Don't lose your equity. The longer you keep the foreclosure going, the more money you can potentially lose. Foreclosure is expensive, and only the attorneys win.

## Asset Manager

The servicer or lender may have an asset manager who handles files that are in foreclosure. The asset manager will typically be your point of contact to handle workouts, modifications, short sales, etc. Sometimes, the foreclosure attorney will handle some of these items as well. There is not a guarantee you will have an asset manager assigned to your file because every servicer and lender is different. There is not one industry-standard approach.

*Pro Tip: Don't misplace your frustration. Calling and going off on the servicer, asset manager, or attorney may make you feel good in the moment, but it does not do anything to help your situation. Depending on who you are talking to, it can make your situation worse. You are just being nasty and annoying. Also, the person who you are talking to is not able to help you if you are belligerent and yelling. Remember, you need something from the person you are talking to. Being cordial will get you a lot further than being mean.*

## Other Key Terms You Should Know

We have highlighted a few of the key parties in this chapter. In the glossary you will find a comprehensive list of key terms and their definitions for your reference.

## Chapter Goal & Key Thoughts

### Chapter Goal

The goal of this chapter is for you to understand the role and the relationship between all the parties you will have to interact with while fixing your foreclosure situation.

### Key Thoughts

- Foreclosure is expensive and only the attorneys involved win.

- It is cheaper and easier for the bank to keep you in your house than to complete foreclosure, but you have to be willing to work with them.

- Dealing with a loan servicer while in foreclosure can be a stressful and annoying process, but you must be persistent.

- The foreclosure process is personal for you, but it is business for all the other parties involved.

### CHAPTER 4

# EVALUATE YOUR FINANCIAL POSITION

*Money is not good or bad. It is an
amplifier of who you already are.*
— *Blake Hansen*[23]

## The 10-Minute Personal Financial Statement

Before determining how to profit from foreclosure, you must figure out what your goal is. Now that you understand the key parties, terminology, and emotions, you need to get a grasp on your finances. The first few chapters addressed major issues, and it is easy to get overwhelmed. If you feel like you are not grasping all the information and are drinking from a fire hose, stop and take a deep breath. Close your eyes and breathe in through your nose and out through your mouth 10 times. *You got this!* Now continue.

The concept of money management may be daunting—but I want to make it as painless and simple for you as possible. This exercise can be completed in only 10 minutes. I want you to relax and remember to check your emotions because this is not meant to cause stress. I'm not requesting you follow a budget or track all your expenses right now. All I want you to do is make a list of everything you have of value.

In the world of business lending, borrowers often have to provide a document called a personal financial statement to bankers. For some high-net-worth individuals, this document can be very detailed and may consist of numerous pages. However, for the average person, this document can be completed fairly easily. The beauty of the personal financial statement and why bankers require it is because it provides a snapshot in time of the complete financial picture of the borrower. Banks are always worried about what happens to their loan in the case of default. Does the borrower have cash on hand, or could they sell other assets to pay off the loan?

The personal financial statement is not typically a requirement for owner occupants when purchasing their homes. The mortgage lender will typically require bank statements, check stubs, credit reports, tax returns, etc., but not a personal financial statement. Therefore, this concept may be new to you. I want to help you make a quick and easy personal financial statement in 10 minutes.

### <u>Simple Personal Financial Statement</u>

Assets

- Checking Account -       $2,500
- Savings Account -        $11,000
- Retirement Account       $225,000
- Primary Residence -      $350,000
- Stock Portfolio -        $7,500
- Car 1 -                  $20,000
- Car 2 -                  $5,500
- Jewelry -                $6,500

**<u>Total Assets</u>**                          **<u>$628,000</u>**

Liabilities

- Credit Card 1 -          $2,500
- Credit Card 2 -          $10,000
- Mortgage -               $255,000
- HELOC -                  $25,000
- Student Loans -          $55,000
- Car Note -               $16,500
- Medical Bills -          $2,750
- Personal Loan -          $1,000

**<u>Total Liabilities</u>**                      **<u>$367,750</u>**

**<u>Net Worth</u>**                              **<u>$260,250</u>**

Take out two sheets of paper. Label one sheet of paper "Assets" and the other paper "Liabilities." Now draw a vertical line on both sheets. On the sheet labeled "Assets," list all your assets on the left side of the line. Think house, cars, bank accounts, retirement accounts, pensions, cryptocurrency, stocks, monthly Social Security income, monthly retirement income, annuities, jewelry, and collectibles. For ease, let's limit this to items worth at least $1,000 in value. On the right side of the page, add the value of each of the items you listed on the left side. For jewelry and collectibles, please be conservative on value, as the market for these items changes frequently. If you don't know the value of your property, we will discuss this in the next chapter. For now, you can use 80% of the Zillow value. It is better to underestimate than overestimate, as you can always adjust later. Now tally up the total on the bottom of the page.

Do this same exercise for the "Liabilities" page. On the left side of the page, write down all your liabilities—think home mortgages, HOA bills, medical bills, credit card balances, car notes, student loans, personal tax bills, judgments, child support monthly payments, personal loan payments, etc. On the right side, write down the total outstanding balance on these accounts. Now calculate the total at the bottom.

The final step is subtracting your asset total from your liability total.

What number did you get?

How do you feel?

Did the number surprise you?

Is the number positive or negative?

Are you richer or less wealthy than you thought?

If your net worth is not where you want it to be or is negative, I want to remind you that this is just a brief moment in time. It is easy to have hope when things are going well and your net worth is high. However, I need you to have hope and faith even if your net worth is negative and things are spinning out of control. This net worth number does not define you. What matters is that you believe things are going to work in your favor. What matters is that you have hope and are willing to work toward the future you desire. What defines you is not what got you to this point; it is what you do next.

Regardless of how you feel, the important thing is *now you know.* You have the information to make a better decision about what you need to do next.

## Action Items

If your net worth is positive, great! That means you currently have more assets than liabilities. Your stuff is worth more than you owe on it. This also means that if you can seriously evaluate your financial position, you may have the ability to cure your foreclosure issue with the resources already at your disposal. You will now have to do the additional work to identify what areas you can pull from or alter to get the money you need to handle the current issue.

If your net worth is negative, don't be discouraged. This is a snapshot in time and not the end. However, you have to ask yourself a few tough questions:

- How did I get here?

- What does my personal financial statement show I value?

- What can I do differently moving forward to improve this number?

- What is the most important thing I can do in the next 30 days to make progress toward my financial goals?

In subsequent chapters, we will evaluate how to handle foreclosure regardless of where you are on the financial spectrum.

This personal financial statement exercise is something that I do multiple times a year. It's not that I care so much about the number; it's a gauge to let me know if I am making progress toward my goals or not. I recommend that you start completing this exercise a minimum of twice a year and track your progress. You will be fascinated by how things can positively change over time when you track and monitor them.

## Chapter Goal & Key Thoughts

### Chapter Goal

The goal of this chapter is to help you quickly identify your net worth. This information is very helpful as you make decisions regarding foreclosure.

### Key Thoughts

- Knowing the amount of money you have available allows you to quickly determine the best strategy to keep or profit from your home.

- Your net worth does not define you.

- You need to create a plan to increase your net worth and track your progress.

### CHAPTER 5

# IDENTIFY YOUR PROPERTY CONDITION & VALUE

*My favorite things in life don't cost any
money. It's really clear that the most
precious resource we all have is time.*
— *Steve Jobs*

The value of the property is very important, but the real question you are after is "How much will I make if I decide to sell?" To answer this question, you need to know the value. Determining value is an art, not a science, and there are a multitude of variables that impact it. Some of these variables are highly subjective and buyer-specific, which adds additional layers to the puzzle.

Say, for example, you have a two-bedroom, one-bathroom house on an in-town 50 × 100-foot lot. The house is 800 square feet, and homes in this area typically sell for $400 a square foot. If someone came to make you an offer on the house, they would offer you $320,000. However, if a builder wanted to buy that property from you, they could potentially offer you $350,000 if their plan was to build a new house that was 3,500 square feet. If you assume their cost to build a new home is $250 per square foot, that would be $875,000 (3,500 sq. ft. × $250) + $350,000 (builder purchase price) = $1,225,000. The builder would then sell the property for $1,400,000 (3,500 sq. ft. × $400) and make a potential profit of $175,000 before real estate broker fees and closing costs.

However, in this same example, if the cost for the builder to build were $300 per square foot, they would potentially offer you significantly less than the other homebuyer. The builder would have to offer you $175,000 to make the same profit they were going to make in the above example. (3,500 sq. ft. × $300) = $1,050,000 + $175,000 (purchase price). = $175,000 profit.

### **Property Details**

| | |
|---|---|
| Size: | 800 square feet |
| Value: | $400 per square foot |

| | |
|---|---|
| Home Builder Offer 1 | |
| Offer Price: | **$350,000** |
| Building Cost: | ***$250 per square foot*** |
| New Home Size | 3,500 square feet |
| New Home Cost | $875,000 |
| Total Builder Cost | $1,225,000 |
| Projected Sales Price | $1,400,000 |

| | |
|---|---|
| Projected Profit | **$175.000** |

Home Builder Offer 2

| | |
|---|---|
| Offer Price: | **$175,000** |
| Building Cost: | ***$300 per square foot*** |
| New Home Size | 3,500 square feet. |
| New Home Cost | $1,050,000 |
| Total Builder Cost | $1,225,000 |
| Projected Sales Price | $1,400,000 |

| | |
|---|---|
| Projected Profit | **$175.000** |

This quick example shows you why it is very important to understand early in this process what the market is willing to pay you for your property. It does not matter what the value will be in the future. What matters is how much you can get in your pocket in the next 30–120 days and, most importantly, before the foreclosure sale.

## Property Condition

When you are comparing your home to other properties that have recently sold, you need to make sure the condition is the same. When I speak about property condition, I am talking about two separate things. The most common and easiest to ascertain is the physical property condition. The second and potentially more important is the legal property condition and what is impacting the title. We will address physical property condition first.

## Physical Property Condition

When evaluating the condition of your property, you need to understand a few different things. You are not the same as everyone else. There are things that you may think are a big deal—maybe they are, and maybe they aren't. And there are things that you may think are little issues, but they may be big problems.

I've gone into houses where the family was living with over 10 different pets, and everyone was comfortable with it. This would be a big problem for me because I have allergies and have to take Benadryl any time I come in contact with cats. Although I like animals, I can notice very quickly if an animal has lived in a home. Other people might have a similar experience with smoke odors. This is a big problem for some and not an issue for others.

I have gone into a house where there was dated wallpaper on the walls and the homeowner kept ranting about how ugly the wallpaper looked and how much money it was going to cost to replace it. It was not bad; I liked the wallpaper and would have kept it if I were living there. The wallpaper was a big problem for the homeowner and not an issue for me.

The things you love or hate about your home are not always as important as you think because the buyer of your home will want to envision themselves there. They will probably utilize the space differently than you do. When evaluating your property condition, the point here is to remember that there are different quirks about your property, and every individual will interpret them differently. Don't spend time on subjective property condition items.

You want to determine the facts about your property, not the perceptions. For example, a fact is that your house is 1,200 square feet. A perception is that your house is too small. A fact is that your house has three bedrooms and one bathroom. A perception is that the house needs another bathroom to be functional for today's standards.

I have provided a property evaluation assessment on the following pages. You can also receive an electronic download of this and other tools in the book by visiting www.theforeclosurefix.com. The evaluation chart uses a scale from 1 to 5 to rate the condition of the most important areas of your property. This overall condition report will allow you to give your home a property condition score.

On this scale, a 1 means the condition is poor and the item needs to be repaired or replaced. A 5, on the other hand, means the item is in great condition, it is operable, and it does not need to be replaced or repaired. Your job is to go through your property and evaluate the condition. Then you can use the average of these numbers to come up with a property score.

The assessment should only take 15 minutes or less. Don't overthink your answers, as this is only a guide to aide you in your negotiations and understanding how to profit the most. The property score will be a good tool for you to understand the current condition of your home so that when you are negotiating or talking with buyers, you will easily be able to say that your property is in excellent, good, average, or poor condition.

**Property Condition Assessment**

This assessment works on the 1, 3, 5 scoring system.

1 = Poor Condition / Nonfunctional / Needs Repair, Replacement or Major Updates / Major Concerns

3 = OK Condition / Functional / Needs Minor Updates / Minor Concerns

5 = Great Condition / Updated in the Last 7 Years / No Concerns

| Category | Rating | | |
|---|---|---|---|
| **Property Exterior** | | | |
| Foundation | 1 | 3 | 5 |

| | 1 | 3 | 5 |
|---|---|---|---|
| Roof and Gutters | 1 | 3 | 5 |
| Deck(s) | 1 | 3 | 5 |
| Windows | 1 | 3 | 5 |
| Landscaping | 1 | 3 | 5 |
| Driveway, Sidewalks & Retaining Walls | 1 | 3 | 5 |
| Brick, Siding, Soffit and Facia boards | 1 | 3 | 5 |
| Exterior Paint | 1 | 3 | 5 |
| Water Line, Sewer Line and Septic Tank | 1 | 3 | 5 |
| Trash, Debris and Property Accessibility | 1 | 3 | 5 |
| **Property Interior** | | | |
| HVAC System(s) | 1 | 3 | 5 |
| Water Heater and Plumbing System | 1 | 3 | 5 |
| Electrical System & Fixtures | 1 | 3 | 5 |
| Appliances | 1 | 3 | 5 |
| Kitchen Cabinets & Countertops | 1 | 3 | 5 |
| Bathrooms | 1 | 3 | 5 |
| Flooring | 1 | 3 | 5 |
| Interior Paint & Sheetrock | 1 | 3 | 5 |
| Pet Damage or Rodent Issues | 1 | 3 | 5 |
| Moisture, Mold or Mildew Issues | 1 | 3 | 5 |
| **Total Score** | | | |

## <u>Scoring</u>

100-94 Points - Excellent Condition
93-76 Points - Good Condition
75-60 Points - Average Condition
59-Below Points - Poor Condition

How did your property rank on the assessment? When you looked at the facts and not your perceptions, did your opinion change?

Do not let your biases negatively impact the value of your property. When a potential buyer, real estate agent, or investor comes to view your house, it is not your job to point out every flaw or imperfection. To the buyer, those things may be minor issues. Investors understand that when they purchase a house, they will probably have to repaint the property and make minor repairs. Property condition characteristics that they can see visually like pressure washing, landscaping, cleaning, etc. should not be a concern to you. The onus is on the buyer to determine whether the property condition is acceptable to them. Now, if there are major defects that cannot be seen, I would recommend that you tell the potential buyer about those.

What types of things are defects that you need to make someone aware of? If there is sewage that comes up every time you use the bathroom or when it rains hard, that is a major defect. If there is a hole in the roof that can't be seen or if the HVAC system does not work, those are things you should tell potential buyers. You should disclose things that are not discoverable without a thorough inspection. However, it is not your job to let people know that you would change the kitchen cabinets, add quartz countertops, and repaint the house. They will be able to see and determine that for themselves.

You can also pay a home inspector to conduct a home inspection of your property. A home inspector is a trained professional who will be able to assess the condition of your property and provide you with a detailed report of all the items that need to be addressed and the potential cost of the repairs. Home inspectors are valuable and helpful. Home inspection costs vary by location and property size but range from $350 to $750.

If you decide to sell your house during the foreclosure process, I recommend that you sell the property as is. This means you are not making any warranties or assurances of the property condition. You will not fix anything, and it is up to the buyer to conduct their own due diligence. More on this in later chapters.

## Legal Property Condition

To be able to have quiet enjoyment of your home or sell your home, you need to also take into consideration the legal property condition. What things in addition to the mortgage are impacting clear and marketable title? Has the HOA filed a lien, are there tax liens, are there judgments, etc. The best way to know the legal property condition is to order a title report from a title company.

The title report will inform you of the mortgages, liens, and owner of the mortgages that are recorded in the county records for your home. A title report is very detailed and provides copies of the recorded documents for your reference. The overview page of a sample title report is below.

## Sample Title Report

| Property Ownership Information | | | |
|---|---|---|---|
| Name: | John Doe | Completed Date: | 9/26/2023 |
| | | Index Date: | 9/26/2023 |
| Property Address: | 1234 Lucky Lane, Detroit, MI 48206 | Report Type: | Current Owner Search |
| APN#/Parcel#/PIN# | 14-07-397-025-123 | County: | Wayne |
| Title Defects: | N/A | | |
| Notes: | Multiple tax liens found. 2 mortgages recorded on property. | | |

| Vesting Information | | | |
|---|---|---|---|
| Grantee(s)/Deed Owner | John Doe, a single man | Deed Date: | 1/5/2004 |
| Grantor/ Prior Owner | William Mack and Mary Mack, as tenants in common. | Recorded Date: | 2/3/2004 |
| Instrument#: | N/A | Book#: | 25735 |
| Consideration($): | 250000 | Page#: | 212 |
| | | Deed Type: | Warranty Deed |
| Notes: | N/A | | |

| Open Mortgage # 1 | | | |
|---|---|---|---|
| Borrower: | John Doe, Unmarried | Date Signed: | 1/5/2004 |
| Lender: | MERS as nominee for ABC Lending CO | Recorded Date: | 2/3/2004 |
| Trustee: | N/A | Book/Page#: | 34558/315 |
| Mortgage Type: | Mortgage | Original Amount: | $185,000 |
| Comments: | N/A | Maturity Date | 1/5/2034 |
| **Mortgage Assignment History** | | | |
| No mortgage assignments. | | | |

| | | | |
|---|---|---|---|
| Borrower: | John Doe, Unmarried | Date Signed: | 1/5/2004 |
| Lender: | American Credit Union | Recorded Date: | 2/3/2004 |
| Trustee: | N/A | Book/Page#: | 34558/315 |
| Mortgage Type: | Mortgage | Original Amount: | $25,000 |
| Comments: | N/A | Maturity Date | 1/5/2034 |
| **Mortgage Assignment History** | | | |
| No mortgage assignments. | | | |

| Active Judgments and Liens | | | | | |
|---|---|---|---|---|---|
| DOC# or Case# or Bk/Pg | Plaintiffs Name | Defendant's Name | Description | Date Recorded | Amount |
| 01234565 / 1234 | Wayne County | John Doe | Tax Lien | 4/15/2017 | $4,274.12 |
| 98765432/ 5687 | State of Michigan | John Doe | Civil Judgment | 1/23/2022 | $795.85 |

| Property Tax Status | | | | | |
|---|---|---|---|---|---|
| Tax Year | Jurisdiction | Installment | Tax Status | Date (Due/Paid) | Amount |
| 2022 | City | 1st | Paid | 9/5/2022 | $2,468.17 |
| 2022 | City | 2nd | Paid | 12/15/2022 | $2,468.17 |
| 2023 | City | 1st | Late | 9/12/2023 | $3,123.12 |
| 2023 | City | 2nd | Due | 12/30/2023 | $3,123.12 |

| Supporting Documents |
|---|
| Enclosed are copies of the public recorded information at the county level. |

This report will cost around $100–$300 but will be able to give you confidence about the legal property condition or alert you to other issues that you might have to address. The attorney or title company that facilitates the property transfer will always order a title report before the transaction is completed. However, if you have time, I recommend that you request a title report as soon as possible. That way you won't be blindsided by anything, and you can start to address potential problems promptly.

You can always request that a local real estate attorney conduct a title search for you. Their fees will vary, but they might provide you with a discount if they will facilitate the closing in the future. Nationwide title search companies I have used in the past for title reports are www.protitleusa.com and www.baldwinadvisorygroup. com. Both companies can provide you with a title report for your home, and their fees are listed on their websites.

By now, you are probably thinking that I am requesting that you spend a lot of money on inspections and reports. Trust me, I am not. You can complete your own home assessment for free and wait for the closing attorney or escrow company to conduct the title search. That is totally acceptable, and it is a normal way to proceed. I simply want to arm you with information should you need or want to get these reports or in case you are overwhelmed and want the help of a professional.

## Payoff and Reinstatement Quotes

In assessing the legal property condition in foreclosure, it is imperative that you request a payoff statement and restatement quote from the mortgage servicer and/or foreclosure attorney. Many people in foreclosure don't have a full understanding of all the charges that have accumulated over the life of the loan. This is especially true when there have been previous defaults, modifications, or forbearance plans. Having these two documents will provide you with valuable information that is needed regardless of how you plan to proceed.

## Probate and Estates

Only 33% of Americans have estate plans or wills in place.[24] So it is not uncommon for houses to end up going through foreclosure because of title limbo. There have been several occasions where we have spoken with families of deceased homeowners who want to sell their family members' homes but are not able to do so because there is no one legally able to sign the contract, closing documents, and deed. This is because the estate was not probated. I have seen people that have lost homes that were in their families for generations because of bad estate planning and infighting.

I've talked with numerous heirs dealing with the foreclosure issues of their parent(s). In many cases, no heir has stepped up to pay the mortgage and there is disagreement among the heirs about the best way to proceed. Everyone is worried about what they are going to get or how much they will have to give, all while people are still grieving and upset about the loss of a loved one. Unfortunately, this is a very common situation, and everyone in the family stands to lose.

If you are dealing with a property in foreclosure and someone on the title is deceased, you need to start the probate process as soon as possible and communicate the situation to the closing attorney and loan servicer. This endeavor can take numerous months to complete, depending on the state you are in.

Hopefully you now understand why the legal property condition is just as important as the physical property condition, if not more important. My company had a property that we were going to purchase, and we were excited about the opportunity. The home needed over $150,000 in renovations, and it was going to be a substantial amount of work for my contractor and his team. The sellers were excited to get rid of the house because they were going through a divorce and had to sell the property due to a court order. Everything regarding the deal was on track, and all parties were happy until the closing attorney received the title report back. The title report showed that there was a HOA lien and federal tax lien. The total to pay off the liens and mortgage would have made the sellers lose money (bring money to closing) at our agreed-upon price. The seller had to terminate the deal. This wasted lots of time and money for all parties. More importantly, the sellers put themselves on an unnecessary emotional roller coaster that could have been easily avoided.

## Four Ways to Determine Your Property Value

To determine the value of your property, you need to understand what is going on in the real estate market. You need to understand the current market dynamics, trends, interest rates, and economic conditions. If this sounds like a lot, that's because it is. But fret not. You can easily utilize the expertise and experience of others who are experienced professionals to become an expert on the value of your property. The best part is that you can utilize many of these strategies for free*!*

There are four different buckets I recommend you consider when determining the value of your home: internet research, real estate brokers, real estate appraisers, and real estate investors. You can use one or a combination of all four.

### Internet Research

You can find out about almost anything on the internet today, from underwater basket weaving to nuclear and molecular physics. There are unlimited amounts of information at your fingertips. However, the key is being able to find the information you need quickly and not getting lost in the copious amounts of data available.

When it comes to looking at property value, some of the most popular sources on the internet are:

- www.zillow.com

- www.redfin.com

- www.trulia.com

- www.realtor.com

- www.eppraisal.com

- www.homes.com

- Your county tax assessor's website

Many of these websites are run by for-profit companies but offer free information. They utilize tax data, market data, and proprietary algorithms to provide estimated values. They may also provide comparable properties, average prices per square foot of homes in the area, specific market data for your area, school ratings, etc. Don't take the value shown on these websites and automatically assume this is the value of your property. In my experience, these values are never correct. They may be too high or too low, but they are never perfect because valuing real estate is an art, not a science.

## Real Estate Broker

You can call a local real estate office and find an agent eager to provide you with the value of your home. Some will be willing to give you a quick opinion of value via phone, and others will want to set up a formal listing presentation for you that will take 30 to 60 minutes. If you are just calling in to the office and don't have a relationship with a broker or agent, you will probably get a less experienced agent because seasoned agents and brokers are typically busy and probably won't be immediately available.

During this conversation or presentation, the agent will provide you with their opinion of your home's value. Keep in mind a few things. The listing price an agent quotes might not be the final sales price. It could be higher or lower. Furthermore, you have to remember that real estate professionals are in the business to make money and not as a hobby. Therefore, if you utilize this method, please show reciprocity and, in the future, consider using the agent who helped you for the sale of your home or sending them business.

You can find agents in your area by visiting the National Association of Realtors website, www.nar.realtor.

## Appraisal

An appraisal is an expert estimate of the value of something. A home appraisal is completed by a licensed real estate appraiser. This is the same type of appraisal that was completed when you purchased your home. The professional comes out to the house, takes pictures, measures the square footage, notes the property condition, drives by comparable properties, searches tax data, and provides all this information in a detailed report with their opinion of the home's value. Again, the key word is "opinion" because a house is only worth what someone will pay. The final value is subjective, depending on a myriad of factors. Appraisals are not free; they typically cost between $450 and $950.

## Investors

Real estate investors are another free source that can be good for determining your property value. Unlike the other sources above, real estate investors can give you a specific value because they will tell you what the house is worth to them and the amount they are willing to pay for it. They do this in the form of providing you with an offer on your property. As with all things, offers are negotiable and subject to other factors, but this gives you a concrete number to begin to work from. Many websites can give you online offers as well.

In subsequent chapters, we discuss the role of investors in your profit strategy in greater detail, but for now, know that real estate brokers and real estate investors are my favorite sources for determining value.

## Drivers of Price

You understand the condition of your property and have a handle on the value. There are a few monkey wrenches that can distort and further muddy the water when it comes to your property. These factors are motivation, timeline, and complexity.

## Motivation

How motivated are you to sell your house? Is it optional, or is it a must?

Every day, people take less money for goods because they don't want to deal with a stressful or traumatic situation. They just want to be done.

I once had an Acura MDX SUV. I really enjoyed the vehicle, and it was very reliable—until one day, I was on the way to an important real estate closing and my car stopped accelerating. This SUV that I had once loved left me on the side of the road embarrassed with my real estate agent and business partner in the car staring at me with a look that said, "We should have driven someone else's car instead!"

Luckily, we were only a few miles from the closing attorney's office, so she came to pick us up and we were able to complete the closing. I thought about fixing the Acura, but I ended up selling it to my mechanic for pennies on the dollar. It's not that I couldn't afford to fix it, but I had lost faith in the vehicle. The situation had been my fault because I probably should have changed the timing belt sooner, but it did not matter. I was scarred by the memory of being stranded on the side of the road by a car I had once considered ultra-dependable. I was a motivated seller.

## Timeline

The value of your property will also change based on your timeline. If you must sell in seven days versus having unlimited time, this will change numerous things. Ultimately, the number of people who can view your property and make offers will be lower. Also, the type of offers you can receive will be different because there won't be enough time to get traditional financing.

I liken it to fresh produce in a grocery store versus canned goods. The fresh produce has a short shelf life, and the closer it gets to the expiration date, the more discounted it becomes. However, canned goods have a long shelf life, so there is not an immediate need to discount them. Time creates pressure, and pressure impacts value.

## Complexity

The more complex the problem that needs to be solved, the greater discount you are going to take on the sale of your property. Why? Because there are fewer people who know how to solve your problem, and the complexity requires a solution that costs more and/or takes more time. The best analogy I can provide is going to the doctor's office. If you wanted a physical exam, various types of doctors can provide this service, so you would have an easier time finding someone to complete the exam and you would find that the cost structure is relatively fixed within a certain range. However, if you had a rare illness and needed the help of a specialist, the timeline to see the physician would typically be longer and the price structure more variable because of the level of complexity.

This is the same for housing and financial problems. The more challenging the circumstance, the more expertise your potential buyer or agent or team will need.

We once had the opportunity to buy a house in Atlanta, Georgia. The property was worth $500,000 and needed about $100,000 in renovations. We were willing to pay $275,000 for the property because we really liked it and wanted it in our portfolio. However, the situation got very complex, and we were unable to purchase the property on our first attempt (more on this in Chapter 11). The owner of the property had recently died, and his parents were the next in line based on his estate. He had died without a will and had no spouse or kids, so his parents had to get an attorney to probate his estate. The parents wanted to sell but could not do so because they could not sign off on the contract or deed. Wait—there is more. The property was scheduled for the foreclosure auction in three weeks, and it would take at least 60 days to probate the estate. So the parents could sell their interest in the house, but it would not have insurable title. On top of that, the decedent's roommates were holding over in the house without paying rent, refused to vacate, and would not allow the family or anyone else to enter the property. There were numerous liens on the property to the tune of $65,000, and there was a pending lawsuit against the estate of the deceased owner. There was *also* another person on the title of the property and the loan, and that person had to sign off on the sale of the property and was very opinionated about how the situation should be handled. The property was in disrepair and filled to the brim with junk and debris.

Needless to say, the complexity of situations like this is detrimental to the value of the properties. People like predictability, and the more variables buyers have to consider, the lower their offers become.

*Pro Tip: Increase the value of your property by decluttering and getting rid of junk. This is the most cost-effective way to make your house more valuable. When people view your house, the more items that are in the way, the more doors they can't open, the more rooms they can't see, the lower the value potential buyers will assign to your property.*

---

# Chapter Goal & Key Thoughts

---

## Chapter Goal

The goals of this chapter are to inform you about the two types of property conditions and to provide ways for you to determine the value of your home.

## Key Thoughts

- Value is in the eye of the beholder. Let the potential buyers let you know what they would pay for your home.

- Utilize free sources for property information first, and only pay professionals when required.

- There are numerous factors outside of your control that have an impact on the profit you can make from your property.

- You might be a motivated seller.

CHAPTER 6

# RECOGNIZE YOU ARE A FAT, JUICY TARGET

*Facts are threatening to those invested in fraud.*
*— DaShanne Stokes*[25]

You are a target! You are a target! You are a fat, juicy target! I can't reiterate this point enough.

According to the U.S. Federal Trade Commission, 1 in 10 adults in the United States will fall victim to a scam or fraud every year. Reported fraud losses increased more than 70% between 2020 and 2021. The FTC received 2.8 million fraud reports from consumers in 2021.[26] At some point in their lives 65% of credit and debit card holders, or 150 million people, have fallen victim to fraud.[27]

The sad reality is that there is a small subset of the world's population who are the scum of the earth and make their living by taking advantage of and scamming hardworking people. If you have ever been by the phone of an elderly person, you will hear and see how many scam phone calls they get about Social Security, the AARP, vacations, insurance, etc. It's a little sickening, but it is the reality we live in.

Let me be very clear: if you are in foreclosure, you are a target! You are a prime target because you are in a perceived tough financial situation, possibly in an abnormal mental state, and most likely experiencing higher levels of stress. You may lack money, knowledge, organization, information, or a combination of all of those things. These factors impact your decision-making ability and make you susceptible to predators who want your money, home, or both. You also have genuine, good-hearted people who want to help you, but it can be difficult to tell who is a friend and who is a foe. So it is imperative that I lay out a few ground rules.

If you are elderly and don't understand what is going on, if you are young and don't understand what is going on, if you are middle-aged and don't understand what is going on, you need to get help! Call the attorney whose information is on all the legal documents coming to your house and ask them to explain the situation to you. Call legal aid and get free help. Call HUD and get free help. Do not sit and do nothing. Please do something. A list of helpful resources is included at www.theforeclosurefix.com. It's not an exhaustive list, so please, check with your local county or agencies for additional assistance.

## Where Are People Getting Your Information From?

Foreclosure information is made available to the public through your local county courthouse. Simply put, your foreclosure is public information. It's not a secret. Various companies scrub and sell your data all the time. Fancy marketing terms like "cookies," "pay per click," "search engine optimization," "search engine marketing," "impression," etc., equal big money for businesses looking to capture market data. Companies and individuals pay top dollar for this information. There is an entire industry focused on providing financial data and housing information.

Did you ever notice that when you purchased your house, you got mail and calls from home insurance agents wanting to sell you insurance? This happens in the same way that, when you register a new business or open a new personal account, you suddenly get credit card offers. It's just like how I'll search for a cruise vacation one day and, within the next hour, I'll see cruise offers in my Facebook, YouTube, and Google ads. Companies sell information to marketers. Google makes money by selling ads and has algorithms that will show you items specific to what you are searching.

When you search "sell my house fast in Arizona," the companies who paid come up on top. Ninety-two percent of searchers will pick businesses on the first page of local search results.[28] There is big money to be made by companies for providing this public information to the masses. Companies want to solicit their services to you. That is why they purchase your public information.

## Signs You Are in Foreclosure & How to Verify

The most obvious sign you are in foreclosure is receiving certified mail or hand-delivered papers from a process server or sheriff's deputy. However, if you never received certified mail or official legal papers, you might not know. I have met with owners who thought they were paying their mortgage every month like clockwork, but someone else was taking the money and not making the payments.

Some of the subtle signs that your house is in foreclosure, even if you have not received formal legal documents, are as follows:

- Random people continuously driving by and stopping to peer inside your home.

- A spike in phone calls or text messages from people asking, "Do you want to sell your house?"

- Random bankruptcy attorney flyers or letters being mailed to you.

- Strangers knocking on your door, asking if you want to sell.

You will feel like someone is invading your privacy and like the public is in your business. That is because they are. They are looking for you because they know you are potentially a motivated seller. You have a pain point and a timeline. They know the secrets I am telling you in this book. Fret not, because I am going to help you level the playing field by equipping you with the tools you need to navigate this minefield.

If you have received correspondence regarding a foreclosure on your home, you can verify by calling your loan servicer and the attorney on the foreclosure documents. Attorneys have state bar numbers that you can check and verify. Many also have LinkedIn profiles, company websites, and web presences. Most loan servicers also have state license numbers you can check with your state licensing authority. Real estate agents have license numbers and are bound by the laws of the real estate commission for their specific states. Real estate investors (who are sometimes employed as brokers or agents as well) have proof of funds they can share as well as references, websites, attorneys who can verify they have worked with them, etc. You need to vet the people or company you plan to communicate with before sharing any information.

## Beware of These Types of Scams

One of the reasons why loan sharks, title pawns, payday loan companies, and pawn shops exist is because they know that their clientele is in a tough financial predicament and will be more likely to accept terms that are one-sided. Scammers know this information as well, and they use it to their advantage.

There are people who are looking to capitalize on your bad luck. You must be alert and understand the scams that are out there. You will receive (and probably already have received) mail, phone calls, emails, and texts from attorneys, real estate agents, investors, etc. Many of these people are legitimate and want to help you. Even if they do want to help you, though, they are in business and they want to be compensated for their time, services, and expertise. This is fair and should be expected.

However, what is not fair and what you should be leery of are scammers who pretend to want to help you but only want to hurt you. Be wary of the scam artists out there who are there to siphon money away from you, give you bad advice, and put you in a situation worse than you are already in. In the age of artificial intelligence and ChatGPT, it is very easy for scammers to create letters that look and sound official. Real estate transactions are not instantaneous events that must be completed with one phone call. An attorney or mortgage servicer will not call you and pressure you to make a payment while on the phone with them. As I stated previously, the situation is not emotional for the servicer or attorney. If the party on the other end appears to be forceful or is telling you a payment must be made right away, hang up and verify the information. Don't be fooled.

Lenders don't call you out of the blue and ask you to provide your complete Social Security number, loan details, or other sensitive information. Remember, they called you, so they should already know who they are speaking to because they are calling the number in their files and have your loan info already. Foreclosure attorneys and servicers will *never* ask you to pay off or reinstate your loan using payment formats such as Cash App, Zelle, PayPal, or gift cards. The only two acceptable methods are wire transfers or certified checks. You must always verify wire instructions telephonically before wiring any funds.

There are ways to verify the accuracy of the claim being asserted. Also, you should know if you took out a loan on your property and have been making the payments. Secured debt does not magically go away because someone stops paying. The lender may not pursue payment for a period, but that does not mean the debt disappears.

In Chapter 5, I discussed how to get a title report on your property to verify the legal property condition. If you are in foreclosure, it will show up on the title report. If you have received papers from a law firm and are skeptical, you can call the law firm or visit the office. (Keep in mind that, because of the nature of their business, most have armed security, so don't get any negative ideas. They are not the problem and are only doing their job.)

One scam I have seen multiple times is when people pretend to be attorneys but are foreigners in call centers reading legal jargon from the internet and feeding you bad advice. The scam typically looks something like this. They contact you and say that they can help you get rid of your foreclosure problem. They entice you with a small fee of $250–$1,000 a month to be your legal representation. They are not lawyers and are breaking the law by pretending to be. You send them the money, and they continue to talk to you on the phone. They tell you what to do, or they say, "We will look into this matter." They instruct you not to contact the foreclosure attorney and to only communicate with them because they are handling everything. They continually assure you that they are communicating on your behalf with all parties and have everything under control. They tell you not to pay the mortgage or reinstate it but instead continue to pay them their monthly fee. They will even go so far as to provide you with documents showing that you were wrongly foreclosed on after the foreclosure sale. Needless to say, when it is time to show up in court, they are nowhere to be found. This scam is meant to suck money from you for as long as possible and keep you in the dark.

This is exactly what happened to the homeowners on a property we purchased a few years ago. I spoke to the homeowners prior to the foreclosure sale, and they told me that they had everything under control. The property was a rental property, when the tenants told the homeowners that they had received legal correspondence, the homeowners told them not to worry about it—they had their attorney looking into the matter. The couple inadvertently paid a fake attorney thousands of dollars to handle the situation. The thief was out of the county, was not an attorney, and had no idea of the foreclosure case number, the state law, or anything else of substance. The homeowners had never met the crook, been to their office address, or even seen them on a video conference.

Be sure to do your due diligence on any person who claims to be an attorney or licensed professional. They should be willing and able to give you their license number with no fuss, hassle, or delay.

Go to their office, google them, get on a video conference, or better yet, meet in person. Stay vigilant.

Investors love people in foreclosure because you don't have very many options and need to make a decision quickly. Scammers love people in distress because they know you are more likely to buy in to their scam if it helps you solve your problem. "Just pay me three easy payments of one thousand dollars, and all your problems will be solved." Don't believe the hype. No one can magically solve your problem. You will have to give up something to get your desired resolutions. It may be money, time, equity, credit, or a combination of all of those. There is no magic pill to cure this problem, and don't get fooled by anyone telling you there is one.

## Tips to Avoid Foreclosure Scams

Remember that foreclosure help from the United States government is always free.

A foreclosure expert can be reached at 888-995-HOPE (4673).

Visit makinghomeaffordable.gov for other useful tips.

## Report Foreclosure Scams

If you have been the victim of a foreclosure scam or attempted foreclosure scam, please report it to the Federal Trade Commission by going to reportfraud.ftc.gov or reach out to the HUD help line by calling 888-995-HOPE (4673).

You can submit a complaint to the Consumer Financial Protection Bureau (CFPB) online at www.consumerfinance.gov or by phone by calling 1-855-411-CFPB (2372).

## A Word of Caution for Real Estate Investors

Zig Ziglar wrote, "People don't care how much you know until they know how much you care."[29] If you are an investor, you have a moral obligation to treat the party you are dealing with in the same way that you want to be treated. The question should always be if your mom, dad, brother, or sister were on the other side of the transaction, would you want them treated the same way you are treating the seller?

If you are an investor, you are probably not dealing with the same challenges as a homeowner in foreclosure. You likely have the financial resources to purchase property or get a loan on property. Caring for the homeowner in need is your responsibility. They are in a fragile state. They need help. You are there to help them, not take advantage of them.

I'm not saying that you shouldn't make money, that you need to start a charity, or that you can't work to recoup the sizable amount of money you spend to contact owners, find leads, and purchase property. I know firsthand the financial pressures of running an active real estate rehab and property management business. We are in this to make a profit.

You need to leave every homeowner better than you met them. Whether you purchase the property or not, you should care about others. This seems like a simple concept, but money has a weird way of perverting the truth and blurring lines. This is a reminder that caring for the person you are trying to help is more important than the home you are attempting to buy.

Maybe you can't increase your offer price, but can you provide a service? Connect them to a charity? Connect them with an attorney? Send them a reliable contractor? Pray for them? Provide words of encouragement? Be a punching bag and let them vent? Let's think about how we add value to others, even if we are short on time and resources.

Let's always be happy for the homeowner and treat them like family.

## Chapter Goal & Key Thoughts

### Chapter Goal

The goal of this chapter is to remind you to be vigilant about protecting yourself from foreclosure-related scams.

### Key Thoughts

- Foreclosure help from the United States government is always free.

- Never be pressured into providing personal information or sending money to someone claiming to be an attorney or loan servicer.

- Utilize free government resources for foreclosure assistance and education.

- You can verify you are in foreclosure by reviewing the legal documents and contacting the foreclosure attorney and loan servicer.

### CHAPTER 7

# MAKE A DECISION: KEEP THE HOUSE OR LET IT GO?

*The man of decision cannot be stopped! The man of indecision cannot be started.*
— *Napoleon Hill*

A common sentiment I have heard from homeowners who have navigated foreclosure, both successfully and unsuccessfully, is "I wish I would have made a decision sooner." Every time I hear this, I am drawn back to the popular philosophical paradox of Buridan's ass. This paradox refers to a hypothetical situation wherein a donkey is hungry and given the option of two equally delicious piles of hay. Unable to choose between the two piles of hay, the donkey starves and dies of hunger.[30]

What the paradox illustrates is how indecision and the fear of the unknown can paralyze one and cause them to ultimately self-select the worst outcome. In this chapter, I want to help those who are stuck in the middle and are having a hard time deciding what to do with their homes. Full disclosure, I am biased and want to push you in one direction.

Whenever possible, if the situation makes sense, you should try to keep your house. Now, there are numerous caveats to this statement, and you still must consider things like the condition of the home, size of the home, health of the homeowner, financial condition, and whether the home is a primary residence vs. investment property, but all things being equal, I encourage most homeowners to keep their homes whenever possible.

Home affordability continues to be a growing concern across the United States, and it is becoming more and more difficult for buyers to enter the housing market. You have a house now, and the value is likely greater than it was when you purchased it—just look at the value you identified in Chapter 5. Homeownership is important for numerous reasons, and I would like to see more people own real estate. Consider the following statistics:

- The *Journal of Economics* studied a group of homeowners over the course of 15 years and regularly checked their financial information. They found that homeowners were able to accumulate $6,000–$15,000 more in wealth annually.[31]

- According to the National Association of Realtors, "Low-income owners were able to build $98,900 in wealth in the last decade from home price appreciation only. Middle-income buyers were able to accumulate $122,100 in wealth as their homes appreciated by 68%. Upper-income households have built $150,800 in wealth since 2012."[32]

- Based on research from 2022, over 90% of homeowners in foreclosure have positive equity in their homes.[33]

| Wealth gains in the last 5,7,10 and 15 years *by income group* | | | |
|---|---|---|---|
| | **Income Level** | | |
| | **Low** | **Middle** | **Upper** |
| 5 years | **$74,270** | $84,300 | $101,660 |
| 7 years | **$85,770** | $104,100 | $122,600 |
| 10 years | **$98,910** | $122,070 | $150,810 |
| 15 years | **$70,350** | $89,210 | $85,720 |

| Wealth gains in the last 5,7,10 and 15 years *by racial/ethnic group* | | | | |
|---|---|---|---|---|
| | **Racial/ethnic group** | | | |
| | **White** | **Black** | **Asian** | **Hispanic** |
| 5 years | $92,810 | **$90,410** | $141,190 | $109,570 |
| 7 years | $115,310 | **$103,530** | $181,240 | $135,906 |
| 10 years | $138,430 | **$115,430** | $239,430 | $162,450 |
| 15 years | $114,150 | **$107,890** | $174,840 | $92,720 |

Source: NAR calculations

These charts show real estate wealth gains due to homeownership.

Regardless of my personal bias, your situation and goal should always determine your strategy. Let's dive into what the decision points are that you should consider.

Deciding what to do in this situation can be very challenging. You know the value and condition of your home. but you don't know what the future holds. No one has an accurate crystal ball to predict the future. When making a decision on what to do, you have to evaluate the details of your specific situation. Below, I have provided a list of questions to help you think through the process.

What works best for you may not work best for me. As mentioned in Chapter 2, you need to get over what everyone else thinks and commit to a plan that works best for you. It is time to start narrowing down your focus.

Imagine you are hungry and want something to eat. You have a myriad of options for what you could eat and where you can procure the food from. You could spend forever in analysis paralysis.

Now let's use this same example but put parameters around a few things. The constant is that you are hungry. However, this time, you don't want to cook, you don't want to pick up any food, and you don't want to spend more than $20 on whatever you eat. Now you have gone from infinite possibilities to a much more manageable list.

I want you to do this same thing with the process of determining your strategy for navigating foreclosure.

You may feel overwhelmed, but breaking this process down into small, manageable decisions is the best way to get a good outcome. Don't worry about every step of the process. Just start with this simple question: Do I want to keep my house or sell it?

If you have not been in the rental market or searched for housing in recent years, know that many things have changed. You may be out of touch with the cost of housing and rental rates in your area. It is not uncommon for people to think they will be able to rent a property equivalent to their home for a similar amount to their mortgage. The chart below illustrates average mortgage rates compared to the cost of apartment rent over the past few years.[34]

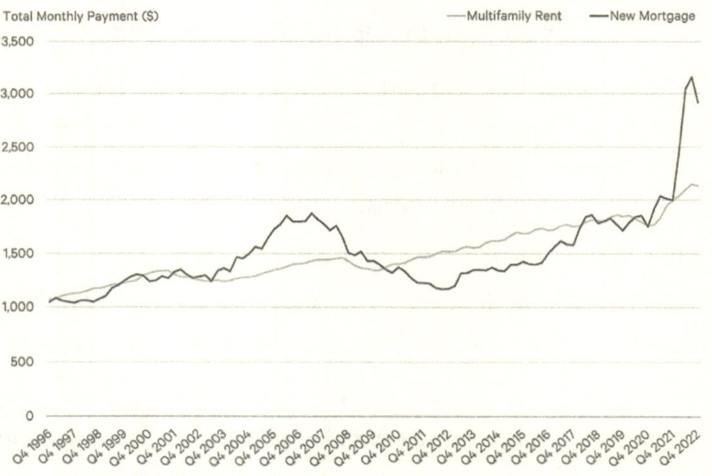


There are two realities that are not true. First is pricing. It is unlikely that you will be able to find a rental location for cheaper than or the same rate as your mortgage. The chart above shows the fluctuation in the two payment variables at given points in time. If you have a mortgage from 2017 or before, it is likely that your mortgage payment will be below current market rent.

The second issue is the availability of housing. If you find a rental you want to lease, there are probably other folks interested in renting it, so there is no guarantee you will get it. Are you the most qualified candidate given your credit, income, and background? Depending on how you have been impacted by the foreclosure, you might not qualify for the rental requirements to lease the desired house or apartment.

You will want to apply and consult with numerous apartment complexes and property managers before assuming you will be able to qualify. Additionally, depending on your geographical location, rental housing could be difficult to find, so you will want to start the search process as early as possible if this is the direction you plan to go. Last, remember that most property management companies charge application fees for each applicant, so you will want to make sure you review the qualifications and chat with a representative when possible before applying.

These are all considerations that you will want to keep in mind as you go through the evaluation process of deciding to keep or sell your house.

## Selling or Keeping—Key Questions

It may not be in your best interest to stay in your home. Don't be quick to put a Band-Aid on a gunshot wound. If you know that your income will decrease and that things are going to get worse, it is better to take decisive action now and put yourself in a better financial and emotional situation. Some questions to consider:

1. Where will I move to?
2. Can I afford a new home?
3. Can I qualify for a mortgage on a new home?
4. Can I find a new home?

5.  Can I afford rent payments in my desired location?

6.  Where can I afford the rent payments?

7.  Does my home need repairs?

8.  Do I have the skills or the money to complete the repairs needed?

9.  How much money do I want to make if I sell?

10. How much do my calculations show I will make if I sell?

11. What will I do with the money?

12. What do I do if I won't make any money or if I have to spend money to sell?

13. Is this the right decision for me and my family right now?

14. Is this the right decision for me and my family in five years?

15. Do I need to live in the same location?

16. Can I move to a cheaper location?

17. Is my house the right size for my current and/or future lifestyle?

18. What does this home mean to me?

19. What is my timeline?

20. Who can I ask for help with this decision?

21. Am I being realistic?

If you have already made the decision to sell, you can skip to Chapter 9 for next steps.

## Free Resources to Help You Make the Decision

If you need to talk with someone about your situation, contact a HUD-approved foreclosure avoidance counselor. This service is provided by the government and is free of charge to you. Visit www.hud.gov for more information. You can also check out our website at www.theforeclosurefix.com for resources and exclusive access to our Foreclosure Fix Family!

## Monitor the Time Clock

When you are at risk of losing your home and you don't have a lot of time left before the foreclosure sale takes place, you are at a greater likelihood of making a poor decision. You don't have the time to talk with brokers, you don't have the time to scrutinize offers, you don't have the time to request the highest and best offer. You have to take the first offer you get from the first individual you see. That puts you at a significant disadvantage.

## More Time Allows for More Options

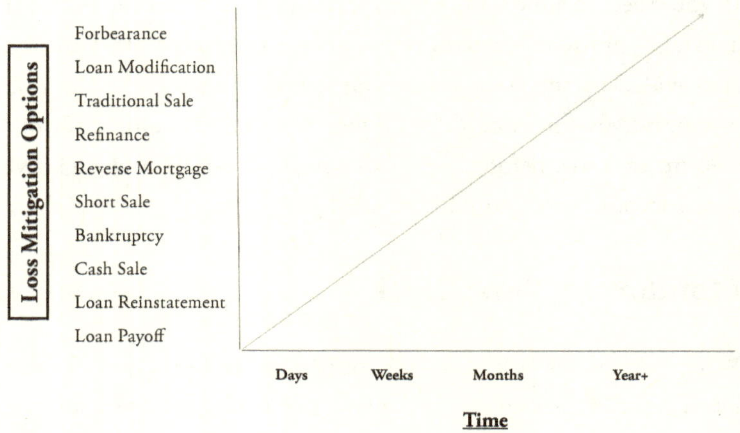


## Timeline to Foreclosure Sale

One of the most important things in the Foreclosure Fix profit strategy is the use of the time clock. Often in sports, when a team has the lead and they are up by multiple points in the last minutes of the game, they will use the shot clock or game clock to their advantage. This is the same concept that you must employ in your thinking about profiting from your property. The more time you have, the more options you have; the more options you have, the more money you make; and the better decisions you can make, the better outcomes you have. The less time, the worse the outcomes.

Time is your most important resource, and you have to use it wisely. This is an important topic, and you might need to take a day off work or spend your nights and weekends trying to tackle this issue. Foreclosure is not a back-burner, "I will get to it when I have time" issue. This is a "get your butt up right now and move" issue.

---

## Chapter Goal & Key Thoughts

---

### Chapter Goal

The goal of this chapter is to force you to make a decision—keep my home or sell my home.

### Key Thoughts

- Don't be like the indecisive donkey who picks the worst option by not making a decision.

- Asking the right questions will help you figure out the best decision for your situation.

- Time is your biggest ally or greatest foe in foreclosure.

### CHAPTER 8

# ATTEMPT TO KEEP YOUR HOME

*Every person who invests in well-selected real estate
in a growing section of a prosperous community
adopts the surest and safest method of becoming
independent, for real estate is the basis of wealth.*
*— Theodore Roosevelt[35]*

So, you want to keep your home; congratulations on deciding! Now let's identify the best way to accomplish this goal. When it comes to the prospect of saving a home from foreclosure, people fall into two categories.

1.  You have the money or can get the money.

    OR

2.  You don't have the money and can't get the money.

Below, I outline strategies for both categories.

## Money Options

If you have the money in the bank and can pay off or reinstate your loan, you are in a better position than most. However, for those who need to raise money, this is not the time to be shy. You need to look under every rock and couch cushion to find the money. Look back at the personal financial statement you made in Chapter 4. If you have a positive net worth, then you have the means to find all or some of the money needed if you think creatively. A few common things we have seen people do are as follows:

- Contact family and friends and request assistance.

- Sell extra stuff—cars, clothes, boats, businesses, rental homes, collectibles, jewelry, stocks, etc.

- Ask your place of worship, community action agencies, or local groups for assistance.

- Investigate government homeowner assistance programs.

- Take out a loan or early disbursement from your 401(k)/ retirement account. (Please check with your accountant or employer about the tax consequences related to this approach.)

- Consider taking out a second mortgage if you have enough equity and time.

- Consider a personal unsecured loan or credit card cash advance. (This is my least favorite strategy because it comes with high fees and adds another payment to your monthly budget.)

If you're looking at this list of possible sources of money and you say, "I would never do that," then you are not serious about keeping your house. If your house is as valuable as you think it is and you want to stay in it, you will have to get the capital from somewhere to catch up the loan or work toward a modification. Since a modification is not guaranteed, you need to have alternative options.

## Pay Off Your Current Loan

This might seem like a no-brainer, but if you have the financial capacity or have financial friends who are willing to help you, you should pay off the loan. Sometimes, people are so busy that they forget to make payments, or they have life events that do not allow them to physically make monthly payments. They have the ability to pay off the loan but decide to keep it for any of a myriad of reasons. You may just want to pay it off once and for all and be done with it instead of forgetting to make the payments.

## Refinance

Pay off the existing loan and start a new one. This option may be difficult if your credit is severely damaged, if you don't have significant time before the foreclosure sale, or if the property condition is poor. However, if these are not mitigating factors, you might benefit from a new loan.

## Reinstate Your Mortgage—Catch Up Your Payments

Pay what you owe, including interest, penalties, and legal fees, and move on. Borrow from your retirement, ask friends, get a second mortgage, figure it out. Find the money and pay to catch up your loan.

## Reinstate Then Refinance

This is a common strategy used when people are not able to refinance the loan right away and need time to rebuild their credit but want to get out of a high interest rate loan or get equity out of their homes. People will reinstate the loan to stop foreclosure with the plan to refinance in six to 12 months once their credit score and financial position gets better. This strategy works well for people who had a single event set them back but have rebounded and are back in good financial standing.

## Mediation or Settlement Options

During the foreclosure process, some states allow for settlement conferences or mediation programs to help the borrower and lender come to a resolution. These programs are typically offered in judicial foreclosure states. They can be beneficial to help both parties come to a resolution, avoiding foreclosure and additional expenses. If you have this luxury and want to keep your house, utilize these opportunities to your benefit. Come to the mediation prepared with a plan for how you can repay and perform. Most lenders are open to listening to reasonable offers and workouts during the early stages of foreclosure to save time and money. However, you don't have to wait until mediation to start the discussion about solutions.

## No Money Options

If you don't have money or are on a fixed income, that is not an excuse to give up. You might have to get a second job or a better-paying job. Most lenders are reluctant to modify loan terms if the borrower cannot show they can comfortably pay the new monthly payment for the foreseeable future. You will want to consider all the options below. The more things you have going for you, the better an outcome you will have.

## Request a Modification, Forbearance, or Workout Plan

You will notice that this section is labeled "request." It is not guaranteed that you will get a modification, forbearance, or workout plan. Each lender is different, and it is very likely that you will be required to fill out a loss mitigation package. The lender takes into consideration numerous things:

- Occupancy status of the property (primary residence or investment property).

- Household makeup.

- Cause(s) of financial hardship.

- Homeowner financials.

- Homeowner motivation and desire to stay in the home.

- Other liens and encumbrances on the property.

- Insurance status.

You will need to provide information and details on what happened and what has changed. Your lender will want to know that the situation causing the default has passed and you are now able to service your debt obligations successfully. Your lender wants you to be set up for success so you won't default again.

*Pro Tip: You never want to accept a modification you can't afford. This will set you up for failure and ultimately put you in a worse position.*

## Sample Loss Mitigation Package

### LOSS MITIGATION PACKAGE INFORMATION & INSTRUCTIONS:

□□ **Loss Mitigation Package Financial Document Request: Please supply a copy of the following:**

- **2 Months of Pay Stubs or Other Proof of Income**
- **2 Months of Current Bank Statements (Checking and Savings)**
- **Most recent IRS Tax Return**
- **Most recent W2s**
- **401k Statements / IRA Statements**
- **If renting the property, a copy of your Current Rental Agreement / Lease with the Tenant**

### General "Homeowner & Property" Questions:

□□ Occupancy status of Property:　　　□□ Vacant　　　|　　　□□ Occupied

□□ How many people are living in the Property (including yourself)? _______________

- Any dependents under the age of 18? If "Yes", how many? ___________

### General "Homeowner Fund & Payment Situation" Questions:

□□ What Amount of Funds, do you have available in the next 10 to 20 days, to apply towards your Loan's Past Due Owed Arrearage Amount?　　　_________________________________

□□ What Amount of Funds, do you have available in the next 30 to 60 days to apply towards your Loan's Past Due Owed Arrearage Amount?　　　_________________________________

□□ What Amount of Funds do you think you can Pay Monthly on the Unpaid Principal Loan Balance? _______________.

_____________________________　　　　　_________________________________________
Homeowner Signature　　　　　　　　　　Primary Residence Current Address

_____________________________　　　　　_________________________
Printed Name　　　　　　　　　　　　　　Date

_____________________________　　　　　_________________________________________
Homeowner Signature　　　　　　　　　　Primary Residence Current Address

_____________________________　　　　　_________________________
Printed Name　　　　　　　　　　　　　　Date

## <u>Sample Loss Mitigation Package</u>

### <u>Homeowner Hardship Explanation Letter</u>

<u>Please explain the hardship situation or reason for request:</u>

_______________________________________________________________
_______________________________________________________________
_______________________________________________________________
_______________________________________________________________
_______________________________________________________________
_______________________________________________________________
_______________________________________________________________
_______________________________________________________________
_______________________________________________________________

<u>Please check all that may apply:</u>

       ☐ ☐ Disability
       ☐ ☐ Divorce
       ☐ ☐ Death
       ☐ ☐ Excessive Obligations
       ☐ ☐ Illness
       ☐ ☐ Loss of Income
       ☐ ☐ Loss of Job
       ☐ ☐ Military Service
       ☐ ☐ Natural Disaster
       ☐ ☐ Other ___________________________________________

_______________________________      _______________________________
Homeowner / Borrower Signature      Date of Birth

_______________________________      _______________________________
Printed Name      Date

_______________________________      _______________________________
Homeowner / Borrower Signature      Date of Birth

_______________________________      _______________________________
Printed Name      Date

## <u>Sample Loss Mitigation Package</u>

Please take a moment to complete the following financial statement and return it to us at your earliest opportunity. For us to better understand your circumstances and tailor a custom solution to meet your needs, we require information related to your monthly income and expenses. If there are additional contributors to your household income OR if additional parties are financially responsible for this lien, please include this information below as well.

|  | Homeowner | Additional Homeowner |
|---|---|---|
| Name: | | |
| Work Telephone: | | |
| Home Telephone: | | |
| Cell Phone: | | |
| Best Time to Call: | | |

## <u>Please tell us about your Property; Please check all that apply:</u>

☐ I live in this house

☐ This is a second home

☐ This house is vacant

☐ This is a rental property. Monthly Rent: $__________________.

☐ Do you have other liens / loans on this property (please circle)?  Yes | No

      Lender: ____________

      Principal Loan Balance: ____________

      Monthly Payment Amount: ____________

      Last Payment Made on the Loan: ____________

      Last Payment Made on the Loan: ____________

☐ Yes, this Property is listed for Sale. Current Listed Sale Price: $__________________.

☐ Selling Agent's Name: ____________________, Phone: ____________________,

☐ I am considering selling the property (Estimated Value: $__________________.

☐ I am willing to do whatever is necessary to retain ownership of my home.

☐ I need help organizing and/or managing my finances.

☐ Taxes are Current (please circle):  Yes | No

☐ I pay my own taxes (taxes are not included in my mortgage payment).

☐ Taxes are escrowed (taxes are included in my mortgage payment).

☐ My property has a Homeowner Association (HOA) (please circle)?  Yes | No

☐ Are the HOA dues current (please circle):  Yes | No

☐ If yes, my Annual HOA dues are: $__________

## Sample Loss Mitigation Package

### Homeowner Financial Statement:

#### Please tell us about your Monthly Household Income:

|  | Homeowner | Additional Homeowner |
|---|---|---|
| W2 Net Income (monthly after taxes and benefits are deducted): $ | _______________ | _______________ |
| Disability Income: $ | _______________ | _______________ |
| Rental Income: $ | _______________ | _______________ |
| Unemployment Income: $ | _______________ | _______________ |
| Child Support / Alimony [1]: $ | _______________ | _______________ |
| Other Income Sources: $ | _______________ | _______________ |
| Source: _______________: |  |  |
| **Total Monthly Net Income:** $ | _______________ | _______________ |
| Current Employment Status: (Circle One): | Employed<br>Unemployed/Not Working<br>Self-Employed | Employed<br>Unemployed/Not Working<br>Self-Employed |

[1] You do not need to disclose child support or alimony income if you do not want it to be considered in any solutions we develop.

#### Please tell us about your Monthly Household Expenses:

Other Mortgage Balances:  $ _______________ Are Taxes & Ins Escrowed?  Yes | No
    If No, Please Answer, Monthly Property Taxes: $ __________    Monthly HO Insurance: $ __________
Other Mortgage Liens: _______________

| Auto Loan Payments: $ _______________ | Number - Auto Loans: __________<br>Estimated Auto Loan Balances: __________ |
|---|---|
| Auto Expenses: $ _______________ | Auto Maintenance: _______________<br>Auto Fuel: _______________ |
| Credit Cards/ Loans payments*: $ _______________ | Number – CC Accounts: _______________<br>Total CC Balance : _______________<br>* Identify minimum monthly payment. |
| Insurance/Medical Expenses: $ _______________ | Life Insurance: __________<br>Auto Insurance: __________<br>Medical Insurance: _______________ |
| Child Care: $ _______________<br>Child Support/Alimony: $ _______________ |  |
| Total Utilities: $ _______________ | Water | Sewage: _______________<br>Electric | Gas: _______________<br>Phones: _______________<br>Cable | Internet: _______________ |

Groceries/Household Supplies: $ _______________
Spending Money / Charity: $ _______________

**Total Monthly Expenses**  $ _______________

If you come to this process prepared, complete all the requested documents, stay on top of your lender, communicate often, and show you are committed to saving your home, then great things can happen.

- I have seen lenders provide trial payment plans and forgive arrears after six or 12 months of consecutive payments.

- I have seen lenders change the loan amortization from 30 years to 40 years to reduce the borrower payment.

- I have seen lenders defer payments and add them to the end of the loan.

- I have seen lenders provide favorable forbearance terms.

- I have seen lenders halt the foreclosure action and provide six months' extension.

- I have seen lenders reduce the interest rate on a loan.

- I have seen many other pro-borrower things.

Good things are possible when you give it your best effort. Lenders are more interested in your solutions to the problem than they are in what caused the problem. Lenders will do things you would not expect them to do when you communicate and are honest. Remember, the bank does not want your house; they want you to keep paying your mortgage. They are willing to work with you to make sure this happens.

A few key things to remember about all the loss mitigation strategies we are discussing in this chapter. **These are very important.**

1. Make your request in every way available. Email it, fax it, and mail it certified.

2. Communicate with the servicer to make sure they received your information and it is being processed. (Go back to the lender communication steps outlined in Chapter 3.)

3. Keep good records of all communication with your servicer.

4. If you do not get a response from your servicer after diligent attempts, file a complaint with the Consumer Financial Protection Bureau: www.consumerfinance.gov

Our firm had a borrower in a small rural town in the Rust Belt who had not made a loan payment in over four years. The borrower had not communicated with our servicer or attorney in over year, and we assumed that the property would be sold at sheriff sale or the borrower would file bankruptcy. About 60 days before the sale, the homeowner reached out to us requesting a modification. This was good for us because we never wanted to foreclose, and we wanted to keep the borrower in his home. From that point on, this borrower was very persistent and diligent. He provided our servicer with all the information requested, explained the seasonality of his business, and was honest about his situation. He called every day, sometimes multiple times a day, to check on the status of the modification, and he did not stop calling until it was completed. He was able to save his house and get a payment he could afford. This was a win-win scenario that was only able to happen because the borrower stepped up and asked for the help he needed.

Note: In this book, we talk about pursuing multiple options simultaneously. I want you to have numerous strategies to save your home. However, it is essential to remember that some strategies cannot be pursued in tandem. Some federal and local programs cannot be applied for simultaneously. Some lenders won't allow you to simultaneously pursue a modification and a short sale. In certain instances, you will need to identify the option that best fits your needs and apply one strategy at a time. The sooner you start working toward your goal, the more time you will have to pivot if needed.

## Explore Bankruptcy

Filing for bankruptcy will halt your foreclosure situation immediately! However, bankruptcy without a good plan is just a delay tactic. It may be an often used and highly effective delay tactic, but it is a delay tactic, nonetheless.

If you do decide to file bankruptcy, understanding your ideal goals and desired future state is always beneficial because your decisions will have long-term, irreversible implications on your credit, ability to borrow, and future.

Bankruptcy is a federal legal proceeding that helps debtors with financial difficulties get relief. The goal of bankruptcy is a fresh start through either discharge of certain debts or repayment of debt through the bankruptcy. Bankruptcy begins with the filing of a petition. The bankruptcy includes all debts prior to the petition. Once a debtor files a bankruptcy petition, the automatic stay prevents creditors from taking action to collect debts from the debtor.[36]

For individual bankruptcy filers, there are two common types of bankruptcy: Chapter 7 and Chapter 13. The high-level difference is that Chapter 7 liquidates debt while Chapter 13 restructures debt. This oversimplifies a complex and nuanced topic, but hopefully it gets you thinking in the right direction.

Although this· book is about dealing with a mortgage foreclosure, bankruptcy might be an option you explore if you have large amounts of debt and are looking for a financial reset. Bankruptcy will not extinguish all debts and liabilities. However, it can provide temporary relief and allow an opportunity to bring all your creditors to the bargaining table.

This book cannot begin to explore the topic of bankruptcy in its specificity. Suffice it to say if you want to explore bankruptcy and be successful at it, contact a legal professional registered with your state bar and consult them for their guidance. Don't go at it alone unless you are well-versed in the subject matter and have the time and aptitude to respect the courts. Lenders get very annoyed with borrowers who use bankruptcy to play games and stall the foreclosure process. Additionally, bankruptcy racks up large legal bills that the borrower will ultimately have to pay back. In short, playing these games causes you to lose money.

***Pro Tip: When picking an attorney, contractor, or vendor, be sure to confirm pricing and get a detailed quote in writing. You want an attorney you feel comfortable with and who specializes in bankruptcy.***

## Bankruptcy Misconceptions

- Only poor people file for bankruptcy.

- Only irresponsible people file for bankruptcy.

- Only lazy people file for bankruptcy.

- Your credit will be ruined forever if you file bankruptcy.

- The courts will drain your accounts, garnish your wages, and seize your assets if you file for bankruptcy.

- After declaring bankruptcy, you will never be able to purchase another home.

## Bankruptcy Advantages

- You can halt the foreclosure immediately.

- Other creditors will not be able to act.

- Bankruptcy allows the opportunity for a fresh start, financially and emotionally.

- You can potentially save your home, car, and valuables.

## Bankruptcy Disadvantages

- Bankruptcy is public information. As soon as you file, the record is online forever (see pacer.uscourts.gov).

- The process can be exhausting and will most likely require legal assistance. You can complete the process yourself, but you must be very knowledgeable about how the bankruptcy courts operate.

- Bankruptcy negatively impacts your credit and ability to borrow in the future.

- Bankruptcy could have tax implications.

- Bankruptcy does not stop the government from acting.

- Bankruptcy can be costly, and some fees may have to be paid up front.

- Bankruptcy only protects the filer.

- Bankruptcy may impact your ability to obtain certain jobs.

## Bankruptcy Tips

- Consult with and hire a bankruptcy attorney. Only work with an attorney who specializes in bankruptcy.

- Listen to your bankruptcy attorney's advice and tell them everything about your financial situation. You don't want your attorney to be blindsided.

- Utilize the personal financial statement you created in Chapter 4 to generate a detailed list of what you own and how much you owe.

- When contemplating bankruptcy, don't transfer assets to friends or family without consulting your attorney. Don't try to hide assets.

- Before filing bankruptcy, do not take out new loans or pay down all your bills.

## Bankruptcy Games

Most people are familiar with Chapter 7 and Chapter 13 bankruptcies. What about Chapter 20 or Chapter 31 bankruptcy? Yes, they do exist, but they are frowned upon. Chapter 20 bankruptcy is when someone files for Chapter 7 and Chapter 13 bankruptcy. Chapter 31 bankruptcy is when someone files Chapter 7, Chapter 11, and Chapter 13 bankruptcy. These tactics may work as stall tactics, but they are dubious. They don't show good faith by a debtor. They also cost the borrower, lender, and courts additional money. If you attempt to use tactics like this to buy time and make the lender lose money, the lender will be less likely to negotiate. Just as investors should not take advantage of people, you as a homeowner should have the same decency. Please don't waste the courts' time, as they are already backlogged and overburdened.

Also, by doing so, you are increasing your bill. Your lender(s) and creditors must now pay their attorneys to file proof of claims and communicate with the bankruptcy courts. All or most of these costs are passed back to you and added to your mortgage balance.

Another game I have seen couples play is filing bankruptcy back and forth. One spouse files for bankruptcy and gets it dismissed, then the other spouse files and does the same thing. This goes on repeatedly and becomes a legal nightmare for the lender.

Some desperate people resort to legal gymnastics as their only option, with the goal being to buy more time. I understand this, but I hope this book will provide you with other options that you can explore. Ultimately, no one can stop you from going the legal gymnastics route or force you to do anything. I am making you aware that this can be a costly game to play.

## Other Options

### Reverse Mortgages/Home Equity Conversion Mortgages

If you qualify for a HECM (home equity conversion mortgage), also commonly known as a reverse mortgage, this might be a good way to save your home. To qualify, you typically must be 62 years of age or older, and your home must be in good condition with equity.[37] You can contact a local mortgage broker to inquire about options and availability of this loan product in your area.

### Litigation

Litigation is a complex and intricate subject matter. It is important to reference in this book because it might help a small subset of readers. Most foreclosure cases are straightforward, but a few are murky and require the borrower to seek legal help. If you believe you are being foreclosed on unlawfully, please get in touch with an attorney for assistance.

Before most attorneys accept a foreclosure case, they will review the client's file. The attorney will look at the mortgage, note, allonges, affidavits, assignments, servicing records, and title report. They are putting their firm's name and reputation on the line when they file legal proceedings, and they want to be confident they have good odds of prevailing in the courts of law. This does not mean that people don't make mistakes. Your argument can't be "They told me I don't owe the money." It has to be concrete and valid.

We once had a mortgage note in Kentucky. The borrower was delinquent and had not paid the mortgage in numerous years. Our company reached out to the borrower via our servicer and attorneys multiple times, but to no avail. We unfortunately decided to start the foreclosure process. About 90 days into the foreclosure process, the borrower's attorney contacted us and pointed out to our legal counsel that the foreclosure was invalid due to the statute of limitations. Our attorney agreed with the findings, so we had to dismiss the foreclosure and record a mortgage satisfaction. People make mistakes every day, so it is not impossible that someone may have missed something in your case.

However, you need to understand that if you have not paid your mortgage, you owe the money and should not be looking for a legal loophole out of the situation. Playing a game of chicken with your lender can cost you a lot of money because the lender is charging back most of their legal cost to your loan.

Our firm had a loan where the mortgage payoff balance was approximately $8,500. We contacted the borrower for numerous months and finally started the foreclosure. This property was in a judicial state that requires mediation, and the foreclosure process can take a very long time. During this long process, our attorney communicated back and forth with the borrower's attorney. The borrower made numerous unreasonable requests and various legal motions, and our legal team spent many hours responding. After over 18 months, the legal fees for the borrower on the loan were over $11,500. Now the borrower's payoff amount was over $20,000, which was in addition to all the legal expenses she paid her attorney. Ensure that you have a strong case if you want to go the litigation route.

In attorney Troy Doucet's book *27 Legal Defenses to Foreclosure*, he lays out the following items as litigation strategies.

- Lack of standing

- Lack of note enforceability

- Lack of mortgage enforceability

- Improper MERS mortgage transfer

- Statute of limitations expired

- Prior material breach of contract

- Failure to establish conditions precedent

- Failure to comply with FHA pre-foreclosure requirements

- Mortgage or note not attached to complaint

- Failure to mitigate damages

- Insufficiency of process

- Real Estate Settlement Procedures Act Violations

- Violations of Fair Debt Collection Practices Act

- Violations of Fair Credit Reporting Act

- Unconscionability

- Failure to state a claim upon which relief can be granted

- Bankruptcy

- Violations of Equal Credit Opportunity Act

- Truth in Lending Act violations for damages

- Failure to provide a correct notice of the right to rescind

- Truth in Lending Act violations enabling rescission

- Violations of TILA higher-priced mortgage loans

- Violations of Home Ownership and Equity Protection Act

- Failure to join indispensable parties[38]

All these strategies are very nuanced, and it takes a licensed and experienced professional to unpack them and explore the viability of your legal argument.

As with bankruptcy filings, people identify ways to utilize the courts to delay the foreclosure or postpone the foreclosure process. One common stall tactic I see is using the term "sovereign citizen defense." Specifically, people claim that they are not citizens and don't have to comply with the rules or laws of the land. They file numerous motions that take months to be heard by the courts and ultimately can delay the foreclosure process for numerous years. This is interesting because weren't they a sovereign citizen when they received the loan and agreed to repay it? So now that they have the house and got the money from a lender to buy it, they want to claim that they don't have to follow the rules of the land. When those same rules served them a benefit, they made sense to them. Now they don't. Respect the courts and don't try this ineffective stall tactic.

## Lease It

If none of the options above work for you and you still want to keep your home, you will have to get creative. If you can't afford the payments, you should consider renting your home out. You can explore a long-term, mid-term, or short-term rental. You can rent out rooms or live in the basement or guest house and rent out the main house. There are a myriad of approaches to increase the income you make at the property. The nuances behind each of these strategies are different, but a good property manager can help you take over all the management responsibilities and can run cash flow scenarios for you to help you make an informed decision. If you are living on the property, you won't need a property manager but should educate yourself on being a landlord.

There are also numerous fintech companies that have entered the real estate market to provide solutions for homeowners in foreclosure. These companies offer you money in exchange for some of the future equity in your home. You stay in your home, make monthly payments to the company, and can buy out their equity in the future should you choose to do so. I don't have any personal experience with any of the companies that provide this type of service, but I am bringing this to your attention because I want you to explore all available options. However, until I have direct experience with a credible company, I can't provide any recommendations.

---

# Chapter Goal & Key Thoughts

---

## Chapter Goal

The goal of this chapter is to force you to open your eyes to the multitude of ways you can keep your house. There is a plethora of options to explore, and one or multiple can fit your needs.

## Key Thoughts

- You need to be prepared and honest with the bank when seeking to modify your mortgage debt.

- Bankruptcy will stop a foreclosure action immediately.

- Seek advice from an experienced attorney before pursuing bankruptcy or litigation.

### CHAPTER 9

# KNOW THY SELF AND THY POTENTIAL BUYERS

*If you know the enemy and know yourself, you need not fear the result of a hundred battles. If you know yourself but not the enemy, for every victory gained you will also suffer a defeat. If you know neither the enemy nor yourself, you will succumb in every battle.*
— *Sun Tzu*, The Art of War[39]

E ven if you have decided to keep your home, it is important that you take time to gauge your emotions. Foreclosure is a stressful event, and deciding what to do next does not absolve you from the hard work needed to bring about your desired outcome. To keep your house, there is more work to be done, and you are 100% capable of doing it.

This process can be long and arduous, and every step can feel like the twist and turn of a roller-coaster ride. This makes it especially important to celebrate the victories, no matter how big or small they are! Deciding to keep your house is a victory— you've made a decision. Other decisions could be choosing to file for bankruptcy or trying to work through a modification process. There are a lot of battles along the journey, and it's easy to get stressed out and frustrated. It's important to stay in the moment and focus on the matter at hand.

I believe in you. The whole Foreclosure Fix Family believes in you! It's important that you have a community that will help you as you rebound and rebuild. You shouldn't try to eat an elephant in one bite. Similarly, you must navigate this foreclosure situation piece by piece by piece.

Access your emotions regularly throughout this journey. Tap into communities that support your goals, and don't hesitate to seek professional help when needed. Whether you are struggling with mental health, real estate, or anything else, there are people who want to help, and you are not alone. Visit www.theforeclosurefix. com for additional resources.

## You Are a Motivated Seller

There are times when someone doesn't just want to sell a property, they *need* to sell. If you are in foreclosure and you don't plan to keep your home, you are a motivated seller. You have something of value that you want to get rid of, and there is a ticking clock. Every buyer likes a motivated seller. For a buyer, a motivated seller often presents the opportunity to capitalize on the range of emotions I addressed in Chapter 1.

Buyers perceive that you are in distress because the foreclosure information is public record. When you combine this with other potential financial troubles, incessant phone calls and text messages, and stress, you have the perfect recipe for motivation. People get tired and just want the situation to be over.

Why would somebody sell their house for less than what it's worth? They would do it because they have a problem, and the first solution presented to solve the problem wins. I've done that before, and people do it every day.

I once owned a nice house in College Park, Georgia. I listed the property for rent and hastily ended up selecting a single guy with good credit but limited rental history. He was excited to move in and paid the deposit and first month's rent with no problems. However, when the second month came around, he was two weeks late. By the time the third month came around, he stopped paying altogether. He stopped answering my calls and text messages. I ultimately had to file for eviction.

While waiting on the courts to serve the tenant, I drove by the house. I did not like what I saw. I had rented the property to a single tenant, but it looked like I had rented it to a college fraternity. There were numerous cars and various people at the house during the middle of a weekday. After more due diligence, I found out that one of the occupants was actively involved in the marijuana industry. Although this is acceptable in many states today, it was illegal when this story happened. I was scared and scarred. I let the sheriff evict the tenants and sold the house as quickly as I could to the first person I could. I could easily have gotten $25,000–$35,000 more if I had waited to sell the house on the open market, and I could have gotten even more if I had kept it. However, I was a motivated seller.

Don't make the same mistake I did. Being a motivated seller does not mean you have to take significantly less than what your property is worth and get ripped off. If you follow the steps I outline in this chapter, you will be able to use your motivation to profit.

## Two Types of Buyers

Some homeowners have never been sellers, so dealing with buyers may be a new and different experience for you, especially depending on what type of buyer you are dealing with. The Foreclosure Fix strategy challenges you to field offers from multiple sources to receive the max value for your property.

Typically, there are two types of buyers for a property: the owner-occupant buyer and the investor.

## Owner-Occupant

The owner-occupant buyer is exactly what it sounds like: the person buying your home intends to occupy the property. They want this to be their personal residence, and therefore they may not care about paying the full market value for the property. They care about the location, neighborhood, and property itself. They are motivated by what their future looks like with the property, not what the perceived market value is. They are emotional about the property, which always works to your advantage as a seller.

Do you remember the first time you walked through your current home? Do you remember when your contract was accepted and the feelings you had about the property? You had already started picking out and placing the furniture before the ink was dry and the loan was approved. Homeownership is an emotional process, and owner-occupant buyers will offer based on this emotion.

The majority of the time, owner-occupant buyers are represented by real estate brokers. Brokers provide a valuable service and want a commission. This means that they are typically looking for properties listed on the multiple listing service (MLS). Additionally, real estate brokers prefer to work with other real estate professionals when possible. This does not mean that if you sell your property yourself, you won't get owner-occupant offers. It means that you might get fewer of them because they may not be fishing in your same pond. You must be strategic and go where they are if you want to find them. They are not looking for you; you are looking for them.

## Investor

Investors, on the other hand, are the exact opposite. They are spending money to look for you. They are bringing their boats to the pond you are fishing in and dropping anchor. They want to find you because they know you are motivated to sell, won't play games, and want to complete the transaction quickly. Remember, this is not emotional for the investor; it is business. They are spending money to make money.

## Three Categories of Buyers

Before we dive into how you deal with buyers, it's important to highlight the three categories of buyers so you can know what to look for when vetting potential buyers.

- **The Snake:** Wants to take advantage of the situation and knows you have limited options. I'm trying to help you avoid the snake.

- **The Newbie:** Is learning how to transact real estate. Not a bad option, but depending on your timeline, this buyer may not be who you want to choose.

- **The Professional:** Chooses to do deals but does not have to do the deal. Honest, respectful, and has the connections necessary to help you make the most of the process.

The snake is exactly what they sound like. They are looking for their victim, and they don't care if you are left for dead as long as they get your house. They are inflexible, uncompromising, and downright assholish. They give you that nasty feeling deep down in the pit of your stomach, and when you sign a contract with them, you feel like you made a deal with the devil.

You want to avoid snakes. These are the people who give the real estate industry, and in particular real estate investors, a bad name.

The newbie is the person who is new to real estate investing. They just got their real estate license or their degree from YouTube university, or they just paid thousands of dollars for a guru's real estate wholesaling or investing class and are eager to try out their real estate chops on you. Newbies mean well. After all, they are committed to prospering in real estate, and they are contacting you to help you out of a difficult situation.

However, what you have to be careful about with a newbie is that they don't know what they don't know. They probably know more than you because they are regurgitating what they have heard on YouTube or in books, but they have not actually gone through the process of purchasing a home in the past. Also, newbies could be dependent on a mentor, business partner, or some other person to help them or to perform a service to make the deal work.

Common things you may hear from a newbie include, "I need to get my partner to look at this," "I don't know how much this will cost, and I will have to get my contractor to check this out," and "I originally offered you one price, but my business partners and I now have to offer you less, although we've seen the house and you have told me about the condition."

This can be frustrating and nerve-racking because you probably already calculated your pending payday based on the amount they previously told you. Also, no one likes more tension added to an already stressful situation. I am all for newbies getting their start in real estate (after all, I was a newbie many years ago); however, you must be careful to make sure their inexperience does not put you in a situation you are trying to avoid.

The last (and my favorite) type of buyer is the professional. The professional buyer is the ideal person you want to work with. Professionals are honest yet humble, candid yet caring, and are open to creating a win-win scenario where everyone prospers. The biggest sign of a professional is that they will tell you to take a better deal if they can't match it or beat it. Professionals know that they won't buy every house they see, nor do they want to or need to. Professionals have been there and done that. They have seen hoarder houses, dilapidated houses, foundation-issue houses, moldy houses, deck-pulling-away-from-the-property houses, fire-damaged houses, etc. They are not scared or worried if a house looks bad. They have seen it before. Hard work does not scare them. What scares them is wasting their time and money on the wrong property. They will tell you the truth.

Professional buyers deliver on their promises. Once you are contractually bound, your problem becomes their problem, and they will use their resources to help get a mutually beneficial outcome for all parties.

# Chapter Goal & Key Thoughts

## Chapter Goal

The goal of this chapter is to remind you that you are capable of doing what is needed to change your situation. It will be hard and rewarding work that you will be proud of in the end.

## Key Thoughts

- You are a motivated seller!

- The two types of buyers for your house are an owner-occupant or investor.

- You need to avoid snakes at all costs. They will waste your time and stress you out.

### CHAPTER 10

# PICK YOUR PREFERRED PROFIT STRATEGY

*You miss 100% of the shots you don't take.*
*— Wayne Gretzky*[40]

## How to Profit From Getting Rid of Your Home

Making as much money as possible on the sale of your home is the way you profit. However, you must realize that everyone who is open to helping you intends to make money as well. The world is driven by money, and real estate is no different.

The Realtor who plans to sell your house wants to make a commission and has to pay their broker, transaction coordinator, and other parties involved in the transaction. The buyer who buys your house will have to pay a lender, a closing attorney, a home inspector, and possibly contractors. Everyone in the transaction will have to be compensated, and the end user will have to make a profit or receive enjoyment from the property. Just because you see a value number on Zillow, that does not mean you will receive a similar number in your pocket, even if the real value of your property is comparable to the number you see.

Selling your home falls into two general categories: a traditional sale and a nontraditional (creative) sale.

A traditional sale is when someone buys your house for a fixed price on a given day and the transaction is consummated. This is how most people think about a real estate transaction. We sign a few documents; you give me money and take my house. Finished.

Although the above option is the most common, there are many ways to relinquish your rights to a property. A nontraditional or creative sale is any method that is not the traditional way. For various reasons, some situations may require a different approach to ensure all parties receive the benefits they want out of the transaction. In these instances, a creative solution might work better to ensure an equitable agreement.

We will first address the traditional approach.

## Four Traditional Ways to Sell Your Home

There are typically four ways to sell your house. However, innovation and technology move so fast that in the coming years there will most likely be others. Below, we will go through the pros and cons of the following methods:

- Utilize a real estate sales professional

- You sell it

- Investor

- iBuyer

To further illustrate the differences, we will utilize a sample property with each of the four options. The sample property will help you better understand the true financial impact of each path.

**Sample Property:** 1234 Lucky Lane

**Market Value:** $300,000

**Mortgage Payoff:** $225,000

**Property Condition:** Average

## Utilize a Real Estate Sales Professional

There are differences between a broker, Realtor, and real estate agent. However, for the purposes of this book, all terms will be used interchangeably.

This may surprise you, but not all real estate sales professionals are created equally. Some real estate agents don't have a clue about foreclosure because they're new to the industry, while others have 20 years of industry experience and still don't have a clue. Not all real estate agents and brokers deal with homeowners in your situation.

You want to work with someone who has experience with foreclosure, short sales, or distressed properties. These can be different beasts. Do not be fooled by the person who has the large billboard but has never dealt with an asset manager to negotiate a reduction in a short-sale contract. This person might be wonderful at selling homes, but they might not have the skillset for your particular situation. Beware of the person who has no references and no credibility outside of the business card they give you. This transaction is not the time to take chances. You don't want this to be someone's first listing attempt. Your situation is stressful enough. You want to deal with a professional.

## How to Choose a Real Estate Sales Professional

You want to select someone who understands the demands and pressures of your situation. This is not the time to choose your cousin, brother, sister, auntie, or uncle who does real estate once in a blue moon. You want a professional who works in real estate 24/7/365, someone who understands the things that I have outlined in this book. You want someone who knows the best closing attorney or title company for your situation, a professional who understands exactly what you need done and the urgency of the matter. Time is of the essence, and wasting time working with someone who does not know how to help you accomplish your goal is foolish. Doing so will ultimately put you in a worse position and doesn't strengthen your negotiating power.

These are the characteristics and skills you want to look for.

- A person knowledgeable in foreclosure, short sales, and distressed real estate.

- A professional who has sold multiple homes in the last six months.

- A person who is committed to real estate and has your best interests at heart.

- A person who is brutally honest and will tell you the truth, even if it is not what you want to hear.

- Someone with connections and resources to help you handle the myriad of things that will come up throughout the transaction.

- Someone who can answer your questions or connect you with a source that can do so.

## Advantages of Utilizing a Real Estate Sales Professional

- You will have someone to walk you through the sales process.

- Your home will be advertised on the multiple listing service and on various websites.

- You will have the ability to market to a large audience quickly.

- You have a buffer between you and your emotions.

- The real estate sales professional is able to handle the contract paperwork and negotiations.

- You will get access to a network of vendors and off-market investors.

- Utilizing a professional gives you the best likelihood of selling for the highest price.

## Disadvantages of Utilizing a Real Estate Sales Professional

- You pay for their services (this averages about 6% of sales price, but it can be negotiated).[41]

- You typically will have to have potential buyers in and out of your house multiple times.

- Your home will be photographed and put on real estate platforms all over the world.

- You will have limited control over negotiations, pricing, and marketing.

- You will have limited control over contracts and deal architecture.

- You won't know if your real estate sales professional is good until you are already working with them.

## Ideal Time to Use This Method

- You need someone to hold your hand through the sales process.

- You are worried about getting scammed and need a professional on your side.

- You want to go for the gusto and get the maximum sales price.

## Projected Profit Worksheet (Realtor)

**Sample Property:** 1234 Lucky Lane

**Contract Price:** $300,000

**Mortgage Payoff:** $225,000

**Brokerage Fees:** $18,000

**Buyer Inspection Repairs:** $6,000

**Closing Cost Assistance:** $6,000

**Total Estimated Profit:** $45,000

**Closing Timeline:** Unpredictable

## You Sell It

Have you ever seen a "for sale by owner" sign on a property? Well, that's exactly what this is. You are the one responsible for selling your property. You stick a sign in the front yard, list the property on the internet, and let the phone start ringing. This method is very doable if you are organized, not afraid of random strangers coming into your house, and don't mind handling the negotiation on your own.

Also, if your home has sentimental value, you may want to know the person or family you sell your home to. You may want a young family to own it versus an investor who will make it a rental property. When you sell it yourself, you can determine these things and get to know the buyer.

**Safety Tip:** Never let a stranger into your home when no one else is there with you. I recommend that you always have multiple adults in the house when conducting showings as an added layer of protection.

## Advantages of Selling Yourself

- You will have complete control of the sales process.

- You won't have to pay agent commissions or fees.

- You will have the option to advertise on a multiple listing service for a discounted fee without losing control over pricing and showings.

- You can be as creative or selective as you want.

- You have the ability to vet every potential buyer.

## Disadvantages of Selling Yourself

- It's hard work, and you can lose money if you are not prepared.

- You will receive lowball offers.

- Your marketing reach is limited unless you pay for MLS access.

- You have limited support and will have to spend money or time figuring out what you don't know.

- You could get scammed.

- Your sales timeline might be longer than with other options, depending on your marketing and responsiveness.

- You won't have a network of agents, attorneys, and contractors at your disposal.

- You may waste time with tire kickers.

- You might have to pay a small commission (typically 3%) if an agent provides a buyer.

## Ideal Time to Use This Method

- You are technologically inclined and can utilize the internet and email successfully.

- You understand the complete real estate sales process.

- You don't mind taking a lower offer because you are saving money on commissions.

## Projected Profit Worksheet (You Sell It)

**Sample Property:** 1234 Lucky Lane

**Contract Price:** $275,000

**Mortgage Payoff:** $225,000

**Brokerage Fees:** $0.00

**Buyer Inspection Repairs:** $6,000

**Closing Cost Assistance:** $6,000

**Total Estimated Profit:** $38,000

**Closing Timeline:** Unpredictable

## Investor

An investor is an individual or company who buys and sells real estate with the intent to make a profit. When an investor purchases a property, they are typically looking for one or a combination of four things: cash flow, equity, appreciation, and/or tax benefits. Cash flow is how much they can make if they rent the property out at its highest and best use. Equity is the difference between what they pay for the property and the value of the property. Appreciation is how much the property is going to be worth in the future. Tax benefits are the tax savings the investor will receive from owning the property.

Investors strategically adjust these numbers by renovating the property, leasing the property, improving zoning, and/or increasing density. Investors are typically not emotional about real estate transactions. They are numbers driven and numbers oriented, and they are looking out for themselves. No two investors are the same. Each weighs the value of the four benefits of real estate differently.

Sometimes, people buy properties because they live near a location and they want all their properties in a certain radius. Some people buy properties because they are bullish on the development of an area and are willing to pay more because they speculate that the appreciation may be greater in the future. Some people are bullish because they have sold a property and are in a tax-free exchange situation and have pressure to find a replacement property. Some people are bullish because they have large investments from outside investors, and they need to use the capital or else they incur fees and other penalties. All that said, do not worry about the motives of the investors. **You need to worry about the price they are willing to pay.**

Investors often have the ability and resources to deal with problems average homeowners cannot. Sometimes, average homeowners can't take on the sheer expense of a repair like changing a sewer line or fixing water intrusion issues, mold problems, or foundation issues, or they lack knowledge on who to call about the situation and the proper way to address it. What sometimes feels daunting and overwhelming to a homeowner is a walk in the park for an investor. Why? Because if they are a seasoned investor, they have seen it before. And if they haven't seen it before, they have a network of contractors and other people they can reach out to.

When you are worried about the roof leak on your house, the investor is not. When you are worried about the mildew in your basement, the investor is not. The investor will price those repairs accordingly, but they are not worried about it. And you do not have to be worried about the investor after you sell. Your job is to extrapolate the most you can from this situation. All parties should be fair to each other, but all parties are responsible adults, and sometimes the investor will win big, and sometimes they will lose.

I have lost numerous times. It is part of real estate. Investors know this, and you should know it too.

There are some individuals who are real estate agents *and* investors. This is probably an ideal type of person who can help you in multiple ways. I use "probably" because there are no absolutes in real estate. The person who can help you the most is the person who cares the most about you. For example, if I am busy and am receiving nonstop calls and emails, I might not want to work with someone who is in a distressed situation that is going to take lots of handholding and time. However, if I am a small but consistent investor and only do a few deals a year, I might be the best person for you to deal with because I will commit to seeing the deal through. You are not just a number. Always try to evaluate who cares about you, not just the house.

## Advantages of Selling to an Investor

- Typically cash offers.

- Will purchase the house in "as-is" condition.

- Fewer or no property showings.

- Experienced party on the other end of the transaction.

- Can close quickly.

- Flexible in negotiation and terms.

- No agent fees or commissions.

- Easy to find and contact.

## Disadvantages of Selling to an Investor

- There is a possibility of getting scammed.

- You may waste time with tire kickers.

- You probably won't get top value for your home.

- You won't have any control over what happens to the house.

## Ideal Time to Use This Method

- You need or want to close quickly.

- You want to work with a limited number of people and don't have lots of time.

- You don't want to advertise to the community that your house is for sale.

- The property is tenant-occupied.

- You are looking for a creative solution that may not be the norm.

## Projected Profit Worksheet (Investor)

**Sample Property:** 1234 Lucky Lane

**Contract Price:** $260,000

**Mortgage Payoff:** $225,000

**Brokerage Fees:** $0.00

**Buyer Inspection Repairs:** $0.00

**Closing Cost Assistance:** $0.00

**Total Estimated Profit:** $35,000

**Closing Timeline:** Fast

## iBuyer

iBuyers are new as of the last few years. The term "iBuyer" means "instant buyer" or "internet buyer." Their name refers to the premise that they will buy your home with a few clicks of a button. These companies are mostly online and spend tons of money marketing with the goal of purchasing homes directly from homeowners. They provide cash offers utilizing proprietary formulas, big data, and technology.

There are multiple companies who are large in this space, and I have listed a few below. While most iBuyers tend to focus on homes in average condition, each company has their own strategy. This marketplace is ever-changing, and new companies are entering the spaces as others are leaving.

- Opendoor

- Offerpad

- HomeLight

- Knock

- Orchard

## Advantages of Using an iBuyer

- No showings until you are under contract.

- Quick offer online.

- No cleaning or staging.

- Cash offers backed by companies with deep pockets.

## Disadvantages of Using an iBuyer

- Offers through iBuyers are blind offers.

- Offers are typically lower than offers on comparable properties.

- The process involves lots of junk fees that lower the cash in your pocket.

- You must be good with a computer and the internet or have access to someone who is.

- iBuyers are not available for all types of properties or geographical locations.

- iBuyers have very specific criteria for offers.

- They might not close or may change their offer after the property inspection.

## Ideal Time to Use This Method

- You need or want to close quickly.

- You don't want showings.

- You are good with technology.

## Projected Profit Worksheet (iBuyer)

**Sample Property:** 1234 Lucky Lane

**Contract Price:** $285,000

**Mortgage Payoff:** $225,000

**Brokerage Fees:** $0.00

**Buyer Inspection Repairs:** $6,000

**Closing Cost Assistance:** $2,850

**Service Charge & Technology Fees:** $16,500

**Total Estimated Profit:** $34,650

**Closing Timeline:** Fast

## Nontraditional (Creative) Sale

You understand the four types of traditional sales, so let's dive into the other type of sales option: nontraditional (creative sale). A creative option may be necessary in situations where the offers you received don't allow you to meet your goals. Maybe you need more money to restart your life. Maybe you need more time to reside in the property. Maybe your payoff amount is higher than expected, and this leaves you in a bad position. Creative offers can sometimes be used to give you the benefits you need while also providing the buyer with the benefits they require.

The easiest way to explain this is with a pizza analogy. Typically, when I order a pizza, I get it all one way: a large pepperoni pizza. The pizza one way is a traditional sale. However, there are times when I am dealing with multiple requests, and I need to order a pizza that is half-and-half or maybe even split into fourths. This creates more work for the pizza maker, and some establishments won't do it. However, when it is done correctly, I can still get pizza that satisfies the differing needs of multiple parties. A creative sale works the same way. You are trying to address the needs of all parties by being creative in your solution to the problem.

On the following pages, I highlight two of the most popular options. However, there are endless possibilities.

## Subject To

One of the popular types of creative sales is called "selling the property subject to." "Subject to" means selling the property without satisfying the existing mortgage or mortgages on the property—hence the name. It is "subject to" the existing mortgage.

In a traditional sale, when someone buys a property, they satisfy all of the liens, mortgages, and encumbrances on the property and get a clean slate. They get a marketable and insurable title. When someone buys your property subject to, they do not get an insurable title. They are buying the property with the existing liens and encumbrances on the property. This strategy is often used when the homeowner does not have equity, but they still want to get rid of the property. The buyer is trading the convenience of taking on your loan, and of not having to go through underwriting of a new loan, for a potential cloud on the title.

If your property is underwater and you want to sell, this could be beneficial to you because someone interested in keeping the property for a long time can service the debt and utilize the property, allowing time for the value to increase. This is also risky for you because that person you sell to can stop paying your loan at any time, and that would negatively impact your credit. Because you are not paying off the existing loan when you sell the property using this method, the loan is still in your name and still reports to your credit. If your credit is already damaged, this may be less of a concern initially, but in a few years, when your credit has rebounded, it might be an issue for you. If you are worried about someone else having the ability to dictate what may happen to your credit in the future, this strategy is not a good idea.

Also, most loan documents have a clause called the "due on sale" clause. This means that your lender can call your loan due if the title of the property is transferred and you do not pay off the loan. This clause is something that scares most homeowners away from selling their properties subject to because they are worried that the full balance of the loan will be due, and the person who purchased the property will not be able to pay it off. You will have to evaluate if the subject to approach is worth it for you.

This approach is valuable for the buyer because the buyer gets to take over what may be a very favorable interest rate and amortization schedule. Also, this allows the buyer to potentially own the property for less money down than if they were to originate a new loan. They save on origination fees, appraisal fees, and other loan expenses by just reinstating and paying on your existing loan. Many investors use this approach as a way to give sellers more money when they do not have significant equity or when their property is in need of significant repair.

If you have a house that is worth $100,000 but the mortgage balance is $95,000 and the property needs $10,000 in repairs and renovations, a seller cannot take that property to a Realtor and get the market value of $100,000. By the time you pay 6% Realtor's commission and closing costs and fees, you may only have a sales price of $90,000, and you would have to bring money to the closing table. You may have that money, but regardless, most people don't like writing checks when they sell property; they like receiving large checks when they sell property. In this scenario, a subject to buyer may be willing to take over your loan payment and do the repairs to the property because they plan to rent the property, or they have an interest in that community and are willing to overpay for the property for future appreciation and upside. The seller gets out of the home without paying, and the buyer gets to get into the home for less money.

If you decide to use the subject to approach, you will want to vet the buyer very carefully. This person will have your future credit score in their hands and can cause you more heartache and problems in the future if they default on the loan. You will want to make sure the person is trustworthy, experienced, and has the financial capacity to pay off the loan if the loan is called due by the lender. You will want to consider adding language to the contract, trust documents, etc., that allows you to automatically get the property back if the buyer stops making payments to the lender after 45 or 60 days. Although the due on sale clause is not used in every scenario, the lender can use it at their discretion.

## Partnerships & Novations

There are strategic ways to partner with investors or other people in the sale of your home. If you think your house has significant value and you don't mind splitting the potential profit with another party in exchange for their money, time, and/or expertise, a partnership might work well for you. These situations are sometimes called "novations" or "joint ventures."

A seller has one price in mind, and a buyer may want to give you a price that is lower than what you want. The buyer or your broker may advise you that the property needs more repairs than you expected, or you may trust someone and feel that it is better to work together with that person to create a solution than it would be to lose some of the upside and equity that you have in your property. This person or group of people may bring a specific skill set or may add significant value. Maybe they are a contractor, and they know how to make all the repairs to the property, but they have no money. Or they may be a money partner, but they will rely on you to make all the repairs to the property. Regardless of what each person brings, thinking creatively and using partnerships is another way to profit from a foreclosure situation.

Oftentimes, when property is in disrepair, the value is significantly decreased. While the same property updated and renovated will bring a premium in the market because it attracts a wide buyer pool, the property sold in disrepair may leave you with little to no profit. In contrast, the renovated property could potentially create tens of thousands of dollars in return. Situations like this are where a partnership works very well. The homeowner brings the property, and the other party brings the labor and the finances to the property, and then you both agree to split the profit of the sale. You are able to profit together.

A few years ago, we partnered with a couple going into foreclosure on a beautiful house in the historic Morningside area of Atlanta, Georgia. It was a duplex property, and the owners stayed on the top level while the bottom was vacant. The property was in decent condition, but the owners had recently experienced job loss and were not making enough income to continue to pay the mortgage and handle all the upkeep. The bottom unit being vacant was not allowing them to gain any income to help with the bills, utilities, taxes, etc. We structured a partnership deal with the homeowners to bring the delinquent loan current, renovate the interior and exterior of the property within a year, and split the profits 50-50 after the renovation was done and the property sold on the open market. We worked with the homeowners and spent over $150,000 on loan reinstatement and property renovations. In less than a year, we were then able to split the six-figure proceeds with the homeowners, allowing them to leave their home with dignity, get a significant financial windfall, and move on to new greener pastures with better credit, more money, and new jobs. This was a win-win partnership.

If you decide to get into a partnership, make sure to get the agreement in writing. The agreement should outline the expectations and roles of each party, the profit splits, and what happens in the event that one party does not hold up their end of the agreement. You may want a real estate lawyer to review any partnership agreement before you sign it. If you don't trust the person on the other side of the partnership, you should not use this approach.

How do you decide what option is best for you? Evaluate all of them. This is the best way to profit from the situation. Call a real estate agent and have a 10-minute conversation. Submit information online to one of the iBuyers. Call some of the investors that have mailed you postcards. Utilize information from various sources to make an informed decision. The strategy is to get as many offers from as many investors, iBuyers, and agents as you can.

You don't have to worry about wasting people's time because all of these people marketed to you or are willing to spend 10 minutes giving you their feedback. Remember, everyone loves a motivated seller because you are not wasting their time. You plan to sell soon, and interested parties are happy to have a chance to purchase the home.

## Chapter Goal & Key Thoughts

### Chapter Goal

The goal of this chapter is to provide you with different ways to profit from your home while in foreclosure.

### Key Thoughts

- Removing problems and solving issues allows you to receive higher offers on your property.

- There are creative ways to sell your property if a traditional sale won't work for your situation.

- Each sales approach has pros and cons. You need to evaluate what option works best for your situation.

### CHAPTER 11

# MASTER THE SALES PROCESS

*You do not get what you want.*
*You get what you negotiate.*
*— Harvey Mackay[42]*

The information you received in the other portions of the book is very valuable, but this chapter is arguably the most important. This chapter outlines how to profit from foreclosure. These are the secrets the professionals in my industry don't want you to have. Get out your pen and take lots of notes. Let's go!

To begin, let's revisit the story from Chapter 5 about the house we wanted to buy with all the title issues. If you recall, the property was worth $500,000 and needed about $100,000 in renovations. The owner was deceased, and the estate was not probated. We were willing to pay $275,000 for the property.

This is a recap of the facts in the situation.

<u>The Good:</u>

- Value: $500,000.

<u>The Bad:</u>

- Needed $100,000 in renovations.

- The estate was not probated.

- The property would not have an insurable title.

- There were occupants living in the house who wouldn't get out.

- Foreclosure auction in three weeks.

- Could not see the interior of the house.

- $65,000 worth of liens.

- Pending lawsuit.

You can easily see why we requested a large discount on the value of the property. If we purchased the property, we would be saddled with numerous problems that would cost time and money to fix. We wanted a discount to handle those problems and make it worth our time.

Fast-forward four months, and we were able to purchase the house for $375,000 versus the $275,000 we had originally offered. Why were we willing to pay $100,000 more, you ask? The situation changed. The seller and their attorney worked diligently to remove the unknowns from the transaction. They solved the problems that were lowering the value and removed the risk from the buyer (us).

You have to remember that when a buyer sees risk, they typically overestimate how much it will cost to mitigate the issue. This is especially true when the buyer is not familiar with the situation or does not have the team or tools to handle the problem. Moreover, if the buyer does not have to take on the risk, their motivation is low.

This is what the seller did. They moved six issues from cons to pros. They solved problems.

<u>The Good:</u>

- Value: $500,000.

- The estate was probated and an executor appointed.

- The seller could now provide insurable title.

- The pending foreclosure action was stopped.

- The seller would pay off all liens at closing.

- The pending lawsuit from a third party was dropped.

- The occupants living in the house would be evicted 30 days after closing.

<u>The Bad:</u>

- Needed $100,000 in renovations.

- Could not see the interior of the house.

When you reduce the risk/problems, your profit increases. Removing the unknown increases your sales price.

## Buyer Risk vs. Seller Profit

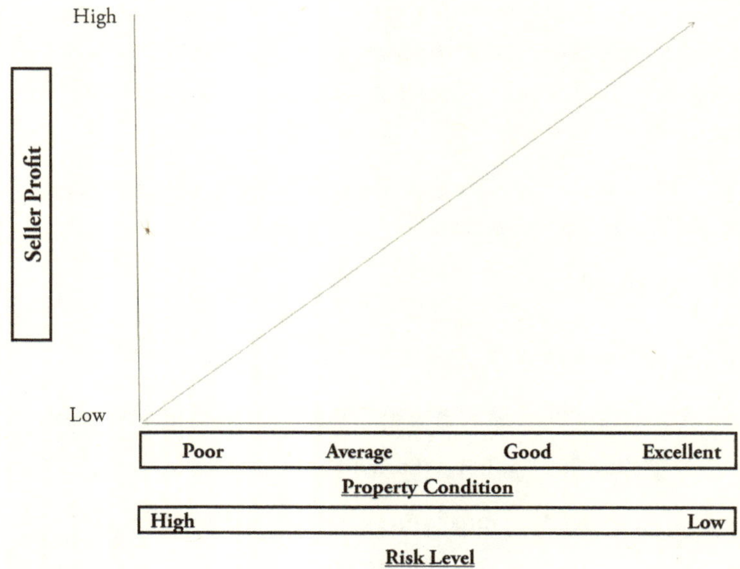


Although there were still unknowns, we increased our offer by $100,000 because we now had more clarity. We had enough information to make educated estimations about the amount of risk we were taking. Any time there is an unknown in a deal, it causes the buyer to think in extremes. Extremes are not advantageous to you getting the best possible price for your property.

Less Unknowns = More Money for You!

## The Selling Process

In this section, I will lay out the blueprint and exact game plan I want you to follow to get your top-dollar offer on your home. If you are working with a real estate broker, they will handle many steps in this process. However, you need to be aware of what to look for and what is going on. It is very important that I provide you with a reminder before we move on.

Don't waste the time of the professionals helping you. In our nonstop society, everyone is busy. We are bombarded with emails, peppered with text messages, and inundated with phone calls. It never stops. When someone is giving you their time and expertise, operate in good faith. If you know you want to keep your house, tell people that up front and let them make the decision to come out or not. Sometimes, an agent or investor will make you an offer via Zoom or FaceTime without having to come into the house. This can save everyone time if you are just looking for back-up plans or planning for worst-case scenarios. Be transparent and courteous because what goes around comes around.

## How to Easily Solicit Offers— On Market and Off Market

Getting offers on your home is very easy. Just follow the steps below. Pick one or do all of them. Just note that the responses may be overwhelming, so you may want to select one or two and add more if you are not getting the activity you desire.

You have to understand a few things about marketing your property. You want to be honest and forthcoming without setting yourself up for discounted offers. A good example is of two car listings on the Internet.

The first listing reads:

"$5,000 for this car. The car runs, but the transmission is failing, and I need to sell it ASAP! Call me and give me your best offer."

This person is setting themselves up for a lowball offer. They are showing all of their cards, and now everyone knows that they can get a big discount.

The second listing for the same car reads:

"A beautiful car for sale. KBB value is $10,000. The car is running, but I'm a little negotiable on the price because it is starting to have transmission issues. Come check it out, and let's make a deal."

This person gives themselves a lot of flexibility. They are honest about the problem and want the buyers to explore what the issues are. They are truthful about being willing to negotiate, but they don't sound desperate. A desperate seller loses in every negotiation. You may be desperate, but the other side does not need to know.

In this scenario, if a mechanic came to check out the car, they might say, "I love the car. I can install a new transmission for $2,000, and the car is like new. I will give you $7,000." This will allow them to make a $1,000 profit when they resell it. Or they may offer $8,000 because they plan to keep the car themselves. However, in both circumstances, the seller would have received more than the $5,000 first listing's asking price.

When soliciting offers and dealing with potential buyers, provide enough information for someone to make a decision to see the property, but not so much information that you are discounting your property before they evaluate it for themselves.

Take these actions to solicit offers:

1. Pick up the phone and respond to text messages. If you are in foreclosure, you probably have people calling and texting you. Don't ignore them; answer them and tell them to send you an offer. Many homeowners think it is

just one or two companies contacting them, only using different numbers. You are mistaken. There are numerous different companies contacting you. All want to purchase your property, but each has a different value proposition.

2.  Look in your mailbox. In addition to all the calls and text messages, you probably have letters and postcards from investors looking to purchase your home. Look at them and call back the numbers. Tell them to send you an offer.

3.  Call local Realtors and let them know you want to sell your house. Tell them to bring you an offer but that their clients must pay their commission.

4.  Submit your property information on different iBuyer websites to receive instant offers.

5.  List your property for sale on Craigslist.com, Facebook Marketplace, and for sale by owner websites.

## How to Deal with Property Showings

Your phone is ringing, your email is buzzing, and you have dozens of people interested in viewing the property and making offers. How do you position yourself for success?

1.  Clean up your property to the best of your ability. Get rid of junk and trash, and declutter. Cut the grass and blow the leaves. Try to make your home look as good as possible. If you are unable to do these things because of your physical condition or time or for another reason, that's okay. The next step is the antidote.

***Pro Tip: Make sure you put up or cage pets when conducting showings. Pets can be very distracting and may***

***turn some buyers off. Remember, you want mass appeal to drive the highest offer on your home.***

2. Schedule all the showings for the same day and within the same time window. You want to create a sense of competition and subconsciously remind the potential buyers that you have multiple options.

3. Inform potential buyers at the showings that if they are interested, their offers need to be received within 24 hours, and provide bidders with your timeline for making a decision.

You want to be safe and smart. When you are inviting strangers to your home, please make sure that there are other adults there. Although 99.9% of people are good, 0.1% are crazy, and having people around can prevent someone from committing a crime and will ultimately make you safer.

I recommend scheduling showings during the daytime and not at night. People can see better during the day and won't make assumptions about your house or inflate their rehab budget for things they cannot see. If you must meet a buyer alone, call up a friend and have them on the phone or on video chat while you conduct the showing. Leave the door open. Step outside while the buyer walks around. If you feel unsafe, call the police. Be smart!

## How to Deal with Potential Buyers

Remember that when dealing with buyers, you want to find the professional buyer. You want someone who is going to make the process easy for you and who will be honest. You don't want to feel like you are being worked over or shaken down. Depending on the amount of interest you have in the property, you might have one interested buyer or 100. If you purchased your home over three years ago, even if prices in your area have decreased slightly, you probably have more equity than you did when you purchased it. According to CoreLogic, the average level of equity for homeowners with a mortgage was $274,000 in the first quarter of 2023.[43] If your amount of interest is very low, you will need to revisit the previous step or consider working with a real estate broker.

The key to getting the most money for your home is competition. You must have multiple offers to know which one is the best offer. Multiple offers could mean 2 or 20. There is no magic number. People have different financial situations and different goals for your home. Some will want to live in the property, while others will want to rent or flip it. Some people may pay with cash, and others will get loans. Some will use contractors to do the work, and others will do the work themselves. Some will renovate everything, and others will salvage as much as possible. All these variables impact what someone can pay for your home.

It is important that you *never make the first offer!* In negotiation, there is a saying: "The person who speaks first loses." Although this is not a lose-and-win situation, the quote emphasizes the fact that you need to be mindful of what you say and how much you divulge. When the buyer asks you, "How much do you want for the house?" you ask them, "What is the most you are willing to pay for it?"

I once attempted to purchase a house in Hall County, Georgia. I spoke with the seller of the home on the phone, and before she told me the details about the house, she said to me, "I will take no less than $80,000 for this house. Take it or leave it" I had not yet seen the house, but from what I knew about the area and the repairs she told me it needed, I was willing to pay $90,000 for the property. Needless to say, I said, "I'll take it!" Luckily, her granddaughter was utilizing the tactics I'm giving you in this book and was able to procure an offer for $105,000. This was $25,000 more than the seller had been willing to accept. She would have gotten $10,000 more just from staying quiet, but she got $25,000 more from getting more offers.

Some buyers will start very low in the hopes of negotiating and coming up to a higher number. Other buyers present their highest and best number on the first attempt. Don't be offended if the offers you receive are lower than what you want. You can go procure more offers, counter current offers, or change your strategy depending on how much time you have. This takes work, but making more money is worth the effort.

As a seller, one of the most important principles you need to understand is how to extract equity while leaving some juice in the lemon. This is particularly true if your property requires significant repairs. Someone buying your home as a homeowner sees intrinsic value in the property. They are willing to pay a premium because they want to raise their kids at the house or because it is close to family and friends or their place of work. However, when selling to an investor, that person is there to make money. You will make more money if you can properly renovate and hold the property long enough to sell it in the open market. This is a fact. However, if you don't have the luxury of time or the skill set to renovate, you have to leave enough margin in the deal for someone else to also make money with their desired strategy. You have to squeeze juice out of the lemon but leave some so that the next person can make lemonade as well.

If this seems daunting or scary, fret not. The multiple offers you receive will give you a very good gauge of the value of your home. I am just preparing you in the event that the offers are not as high as you want them to be.

## How to Choose the Right Buyer

You should not feel bad if you have multiple people seeing your home or if you are fielding multiple offers. This happens all the time in a normal real estate market. Have you ever been to an open house? Buyers and investors are used to having competition. It is the reason why real estate agents love pocket listings that are not on the multiple listing service. The less competition, the better the deals they can get for their clients. Desirable real estate is in high demand, and you want to create healthy competition for your home.

It is a buyer's job to see numerous houses and to evaluate them. If the buyer is a professional, they won't be put off by competition, and they won't care. They will make you an offer that works for them, and they will be appreciative that you allowed them a chance at an off-market property.

As you begin to receive offers, you will want to compare and contrast them. I have provided a sample chart for you to input the important details into. You can download it at www.theforeclosurefix.com.

# Multiple Offer Template

| Offer # | Purchase Price | Closing Cost | Net Offer | Closing Date | Due Diligence | Earnest Money | Financing Type | Financing Contingency | Appraisal Contingency | Offer Expiration Date | Notes |
|---|---|---|---|---|---|---|---|---|---|---|---|
| 1 | $285,000 | $5,000 | $280,000 | 6/12/23 | 10 Days | $3,000 | Conventional | 21 Days | 21 Days | 5/10/23 6:00PM | Owner Occupant |
| 2 | $275,000 | $0 | $275,000 | 5/28/23 | 10 Days | $2,750 | Cash | 0 | 0 | 5/11/23 9:00 AM | Newbie |
| 3 | $286,000 | $10,000 | $276,000 | 6/30/23 | 0 | $5,000 | FHA | 8 Days | 8 Days | 5/14/23 10:00 AM | Owner Occupant |
| 4 | $285,000 | $0 | $285,000 | Negotiable | 7 Days | $10,000 | Cash | 0 | 0 | 5/13/23 2:00 PM | Professional |
| 5 | $225,000 | $5,000 | $220,000 | 6/12/23 | 10 Days | $2,000 | Conventional | 21 Days | 21 Days | 5/10/23 6:00 PM | Snake |
|  |  |  |  |  |  |  |  |  |  |  |  |
|  |  |  |  |  |  |  |  |  |  |  |  |
|  |  |  |  |  |  |  |  |  |  |  |  |
|  |  |  |  |  |  |  |  |  |  |  |  |

This multiple offer template is simple and allows you to easily input the important details about each offer. It is an easy way for you to begin to narrow down your top offers.

Selecting the best buyer can be challenging. It is part art and part science. You have to add up the pros and subtract the cons to get an offer or buyer you like. "Offer or buyer?" you may ask. "I thought I was only worried about the offer!" You are, but the offer and buyer are one. You can have the highest offer from a buyer you don't like or from one who is inexperienced. That may or may not be the best offer for you to accept. You have to evaluate what is going to work best for you.

What things do you take into consideration? Consider purchase price, closing timeline, and method of payment. Then sprinkle in some of the intangible items. How long are they going to let you stay in the property before you have to move out? Are they willing to take away the garbage and the junk that you leave behind, or do you have to leave the house broom swept? Are they helping you relocate? There are so many different ways to make a deal work, and you want someone committed to making a deal work with you.

Don't let the experience of the buyer be the only factor. Review each of the offers you receive carefully. Also consider the nonmonetary items and terms of the contract. It's about the complete offer, not just the money.

You have to be leery of dishonest buyers who use tactics that are predatory to maximize their gain. A professional buyer should be able to help you understand their perspective. A professional buyer is there to help you. Let me repeat this so it sinks in: *a professional buyer is there to help you!* A professional buyer is there to aid you in solving your problem. That means that they might not buy your house, and if they do end up buying your house, the deal is favorable to both parties and it is a win-win.

What exactly does your ideal buyer look and feel like?

- The person you are dealing with is able to answer all of your questions or refer you to the legal or tax professional who can answer them.

- They are not rushing you to sign something that you don't understand and they can't explain.

- They are not pushy or aggressive.

- They explain other options and the pros and cons of those options.

- They are not desperate or overly salesy.

- They can provide you with proof of funds for the purchase of the property.

- You can talk to their closing attorney or title company and ask questions. Specifically:

  o How many transactions have you done with the person/company?

  o Have they ever canceled a contract at the last minute and not closed?

  o Can the company meet the timeline?

When dealing with any person on the sale of your home, you need to trust your gut. If something seems off, it probably is.

If you are in foreclosure, you need to remember to be seasonally selfish. Forget about being liked. You are in a battle for your home, and you need to understand what is at stake. You need to get very specific about the outcome you want, and if that outcome is to make as much money as possible, you need to be prepared to do the work. Everyone can't buy your house; only one person can. You must find the person willing to give you the best offer. This does not always mean the most money. Money is only one of many components.

The professional buyer knows that you get the best returns when you help someone. There is no greater feeling than helping someone during a challenging stage in life. You want to work with somebody who does not make you feel like they are a swindler. You want a professional, not a snake.

## Understanding and Negotiating the Contract

If contract negotiations seem too overwhelming to you, you should consider using a real estate sales professional or hiring a real estate attorney to review your documents and represent you in the transaction. Some real estate brokers will accept a discounted commission or flat fee for their services. A real estate attorney can look over contracts before you sign off, and they can communicate with the buyer and facilitate the property transfer. This may provide you with reassurance if negotiating is not something you want to do. You can search online for real estate attorneys in your area.

How to negotiate is a delicate subject because everyone has their own methods. When negotiating, I believe it is always best to act in good faith and remember the goal. Two people are choosing to work together for a mutually beneficial outcome. Both parties should feel that they are getting a good deal and that it is a win-win.

Your buyer is interested in your house to make a profit or for their enjoyment. Either way, the cheaper they can purchase a property, the better and safer the deal is for them. Remember the stress versus profit chart from Chapter 10. Buyers are used to hearing "no" and making offers that don't get accepted or will be negotiated. You can always counter their offers. A counteroffer is when you reject their initial offer and propose a new offer.

Example: Someone offers you $100,000 for your house and wants to close in 14 days. You think your house is worth more and want to close in seven days but live in the house for 30 days after closing. You can easily tell them: you will not accept $100,000, but you will consider $125,000, closing in seven days with a 30-day leaseback period. It is as simple as that.

Negotiations are a normal part of everyday life and nothing to be overwhelmed by. My daughters negotiate with me every day when they ask me for dessert. I'm a sucker for my girls, and most of the time I give in and allow them to have a dessert. I will say, "You can have a small piece of candy." They will quickly reply, "Can we have a cupcake or ice cream?" I will say no. Then they will say, "Well, can we get three pieces of candy?" And this goes back and forth until we agree.

The buyer wants what you have, and a counteroffer will not make them go away or lose interest. If they do, they were not serious about purchasing your home in the first place, and you need to move on to the next offer. The worst outcome is that they will say no to your counteroffer and stay firm on their original offer.

Don't be afraid to ask a buyer how they arrived at their offer price. They should be able to tell you the calculations they used and the numbers they are factoring into the deal.

Let's continue with the example of the house where someone offered $100,000 but you countered at $125,000. The potential buyer responds back and says, "I'm sorry, but the most I can pay is $110,000." You can ask how they arrived at this number.

They should be able to provide you with a math breakout or calculation that looks like what you see below.

**Profit Breakout Sheet**
**Sample Property: 1234 Lucky Lane**

| | |
|---|---|
| Buyer's Offer Price to Homeowner: | $110,000 |
| Buyer's Estimated Renovation Cost: | $50,000 |
| **Buyer's Total Investment:** | **$160,000** |
| **Estimated Sales Price (After Repair Value):** | **$200,000** |
| Brokerage Fees: | $12,000 |
| Inspection Repairs: | $1,000 |
| Closing Cost Assistance: | $2,000 |
| **Total Estimated Selling Cost & Investment:** | **$175,000** |
| **Estimated Net profit for Buyer** | **$25,000** |

Based on their calculations you should be able to easily see what numbers they are using to value your property and how they arrived at their offer. From this, you can poke holes in their numbers and better understand their perspective. Maybe their rehab costs are too high, or their after-repair value is too low based on where the real estate market is. This gives you the opportunity to discuss how you both see the world and come to a meeting of the minds, should you desire to do so.

You will want to keep in mind that, for the potential buyer, the risk should match the reward. If you have a problem property that is in poor condition, please anticipate that the buyer will want to make more money to help you solve a more complex problem that has multiple layers of stress. You have to leave enough juice in the lemon. However, if you have a house that is in good condition and the only issue is the pending foreclosure, then you can command more money and they will get less profit.

These are items you will want to make sure are included in your final contract.

- You want to negotiate being able to leave the belongings you don't want to take with you.

- You want to negotiate time after the sale to move out if needed.

- You will want some cash at the closing to help you with the moving expenses. (This cash will come out of your profit amount, but you will get it at the closing table.)

- You will want to make sure you are selling the house "as is" and are not responsible for any repairs.

It does not always work out that you will get the max value for your home, but understanding exactly how to negotiate favorably is important to obtaining your best offer. The dollar amount of the offer is important, but so are the terms. Your buyer might not be able to adjust their purchase price, but they may be able to modify their terms in your favor. When time is tight, a fair deal is better than no deal. If you want a better deal, start the process earlier. More time provides more options and better outcomes.

Remember, the person you are working with is not your enemy—they are your ally, and you both should be working together to create a deal that is a win-win (they win because they feel like they've paid a fair price for the property, and you win because you received a fair price). Both parties should be happy in the situation. If that is not the case, then it's not really a deal and someone is getting taken advantage of.

This entire process seems like it is very lengthy, but it does not have to be. This could be completed and finalized in a few short days if you are organized and put forth the time and effort required.

## Don't Make These Contract Mistakes

Recently, we were working with a homeowner to purchase her home in foreclosure. She thought the loan payoff was $150,000 and was happy with our offer. When she ordered the payoff from the servicer, her payoff ended up being $205,000. She had an equity appreciation loan, and the lender was entitled to the profit in the property. Based on this, she was no longer happy with our original offer because she was not making enough money. We parted ways, and she went with another offer. The problem was that the new offer did not provide any earnest money, and the closing date was after the foreclosure sale date. She trusted the buyer because he was a friend of her granddaughter.

Fast-forward to a few days before the foreclosure sale, and the buyer ghosted her. She did not hear from the closing attorney; she was not getting returned calls or text messages, and she was going to lose her house and not walk away with anything. Unfortunately, this borrower had to file bankruptcy to stop the foreclosure. We ended up purchasing the property a couple months later when the seller reached out to us again and explained what had happened. This story shows why these contract items are so important.

Major Points:

1.  The first offer is not always the best offer. It is okay to counter offers.

2.  The highest offer is not always the best offer.

3.  Not reading the entire contract will cause you problems.

4.  Not contacting the settlement agent, escrow company, and/or closing attorney prior to signing the contract will cause you problems.

5.  A buyer not having earnest money is a red flag.

6.  Allowing inspection contingencies that run the entire length of the contract is a red flag.

7.  Allowing one party to get out of the contract without penalty after the contingency period is bad for you.

8.  Not having proof of funds or preapproval is a red flag.

9.  Not allowing the contract to have an expiration date is bad for you.

10. Accepting blind offers is a bad idea.

11. Accepting language in the contract about assignments can leave you in a bad position.

12. Don't try to anticipate what someone is going to do or say.

13. Don't let someone pressure you into signing a contract right away. Stop, think, and get advice when needed.

14. Always leave yourself enough time to go with another buyer.

15. Moving too slowly will cause you problems.

16. Not staying on top of the transaction will cause you problems.

## Key Parts of a Real Estate Contract

It is always important to read and understand all portions and all pages of a contract before you sign it. If you don't understand the contract, don't sign it, and get professional help. I have highlighted some of the most common sections of a real estate contract and their importance to you as a seller.

- **Purchase Price:** The amount the buyer is paying the seller.

- **Earnest Money:** The deposit a buyer is putting down in the event they cannot fulfill their end contract. This is money you will receive if they don't perform as agreed.

- **Holder of Earnest Money:** The company/law firm who is holding the earnest money and will settle any disputes regarding who is to receive it.

- **Closing or Settlement Date:** The date the property is scheduled to transfer from seller to buyer.

- **Due Diligence:** The timeline the buyer has to inspect the property and terminate the contract without penalty.

- **Closing Attorney/Title Company:** The company facilitating the sale and recording all of the legal documents required for title transfer. This company will typically represent the lender if a lender is involved in the transaction.

- **Financing:** The method the buyer is using to purchase the property.

- **Extensions:** Automatic rights to extend important dates, such as closing date or due diligence.

- **Special Stipulations:** Anything else that is not covered in the other areas of the contract would be placed in this section.

- **Disclosures & Agency:** Information regarding licensed parties in the transaction.

- **Assignments:** I specifically left "assignments" as the last item because it is very important. When reviewing real estate contracts, you will want to note if there is an assignment clause. This language allows the buyer to assign the contract to someone else. This is not implicitly bad, but it is something you will want to note. This is also a good segue to talk about the term "wholesaling."

Wholesaling exists in every industry. It is how most businesses operate. When you shop at Walmart, they contract with a food producer at one price and charge a premium to you as the consumer for the convenience of buying one can of soup at a time instead of 10,000. When you go to a used car dealership, the dealer purchased the car for less than he will sell it to you for. That is the same thing house wholesalers do. They purchase your house at one price and sell it to their investor network at a premium to cover their marketing and business expenses.

You will want to know if you are selling your home to a wholesaler. This is not a bad thing, but it is something you will want to be aware of and pay close attention to. Because the wholesaler is not typically the end user, they might be more inclined to terminate their contract with you if they can't find a buyer for your home. This can be especially frustrating if you are on a tight timeline. You will want to consider this before accepting this type of language in your contract.

## What to Do Before Signing Any Contract

You have found your buyer and negotiated the contract, and now it is time to sign off. Follow these steps before signing any real estate contract.

1. Read the entire contract and make sure you understand it. If you don't understand it, ask questions and get help.

2. Take 2 to 24 hours to make sure that you agree with everything you are signing. I like to sleep on big decisions, hence the 24 hours. This is an important decision, and even though the time is ticking, you want to make sure this is the right decision for you.

3. If the buyer is a professional buyer and not an owner-occupant, ask for references.

4. If there is a lender involved, call the lender and confirm the buyer's ability to fund the transaction.

5. Call the closing attorney/title company and confirm that they can meet your desired timeline.

6. Listen to your gut and trust your intuition.

Don't let someone bully you into thinking you have to go with their offer. Some companies and investors are dishonest and see you as a target because they know you are scared, anxious, and in a fragile emotional state. Don't sign anything you don't understand! Read everything before you sign it! If you don't understand something, make the buyer explain it to you!

A purchase contract can be as short as one or two pages. If someone gives you a contract that is too long, ask them for a shorter contact.

## These Are Deal-Killers

This may be a hard pill to swallow, but some people are destined for foreclosure. It's not a matter of how much money you have or don't have, how much time you have or don't have, how much influence you have or don't have. Some people don't and won't see the bigger picture and will end up missing their opportunity to profit. All the information is out there. You have all the tools, but you let something get in the way. That something could be ego, pride, or short-sightedness. Whatever it is, it gets in the way of you having your payday and moving on with your life.

Below, I outline the deal-killers that you will have to manage in this process. Everyone in the transaction wants competing things. You want to be done with the situation and to make money. The buyer wants to pay the least amount of money and get the best possible terms. These are competing forces.

Below are the major deal-killers.

- **Greed:** Buyer, seller, and/or agents being too greedy. They want too much money or too many concessions, and the deal is not favorable for the other parties.

- **Dishonesty:** Any party not disclosing known issues, such as title issues, tax liens, funding problems, etc.

- **Ego:** One or more parties feeling they have to make a stand or be right.

- **Time:** Not enough time to get the deal closed due to lack of communication or outside factors.

Don't be an unreasonable seller. If you have followed my plan and are under contract to sell for the best possible amount and favorable terms, there are still numerous traps that can hinder your big payday—primarily being unreasonable and unaware. By now, you should have taken inventory of your home. You have completed the inspection sheet. You have spoken with real estate agents and investors, and you have a good ballpark of where the value of your home is. You have reviewed Zillow, Redfin, Trulia, etc. You are aware of the current market in your area and understand if you are in a seller's market, buyer's market, or even market. You are knowledgeable—just as the old '90s television commercials said, "Knowledge is power."

However, what can kill a deal faster than anything else is an unreasonable seller. Once you decide what the best route for you to take is and what offer provides you with the most benefits, don't let emotions or minor issues get in the way of your payday. Don't trip over pennies when you can pick up dollars. I'm not telling you to let your buyer run over you or make unreasonable requests. I'm alerting you that you are near the finish line, and once you have determined the deal is fair and you have a buyer, you shouldn't let a few dollars derail your long-term goal. This seems simple and maybe trivial, but when your emotions are high, your savings are low, and the battle is raging, you need to find a way to stay calm and keep your cool. Take a breath before sending that email or text. Wait an hour before picking up the phone and going off. Get perspective from people who are detached from the situation and can be objective. The goal is to maximize profit. Remember the time value of money: a dollar today is better than a dollar tomorrow. Don't let greed, dishonesty, or ego stop your dollar today.

## Time Is of the Essence

You have fewer options as more time passes and you get closer to foreclosure.

I liken your situation to this. After a long day of work, school, and kids' activities, I am in the car driving home with my kids. The clock shows that it is 7 p.m., and my kids still need to do their homework, eat dinner, bathe, and get ready for bed. The kids are complaining of hunger and fighting with each other. I'm tired, frustrated, and have a million things on my mind.

I have a few options in this scenario. I can swing by a drive-through and pick up food, or I can wait until I get home and cook. What option do I choose?

I can make a better burger than McDonald's, and it is cheaper for us to eat at home. However, this requires me to listen to arguing and complaining for 30 more minutes, then get home and cook for 45 minutes before a meal is ready. Or I can pay McDonald's a premium and have my food in five minutes, stop the complaining, and be ready to wind down when I get home. One option is cheaper and tastes better, but the other option is more expensive and solves my problem now.

The choice is mine, but regardless, I'm trading convenience for money. That is what you are doing with your house when you sell off market. You are trading ease and convenience for money. This is not the best option in every situation, but there are times when it makes a lot of sense and is the optimal decision.

In my previous career, I was a management consultant and traveled a lot. I was always amazed that a bottle of water in the airport was so darn expensive. You would think God had kissed the bottle of water and said, "This will heal all your infirmities." The same water I could buy for $1 outside the TSA boundaries would cost me $5 behind them. This is the same for food, phone chargers, and everything else. Why? It's because people in the airport don't have any other options. Either you want the water, or you don't. This is what happens to you when you wait until the last minute to deal with your foreclosure situation. You run out of options and are forced to choose an option that is less optimal for you.

It does not work to have only one option; you need multiple. You should always have options one, two, and three. Brokers fail, lenders fail, and investors fail. You must take ownership of the outcome, and no one cares more than you. It is your responsibility to get out of this mess—no one else's. You can trust but verify. You can hope and believe, but follow up. This is not a "sit back and watch" situation; this is an "all hands on deck" environment. You have to act accordingly.

It is very important that you stay on top of the process to the very end. If you have decided to keep your home, you need to make sure that the foreclosure is canceled and you have this information in writing. If you are selling your home, you need to make sure that you are in communication with all parties in the transaction. You have the most to lose and gain. It is your job, your problem, your burden. Don't wait for someone else to initiate; you get the ball moving. Remember, time is of the essence.

## Chapter Goal & Key Thoughts

### Chapter Goal

The goal of this chapter is to remind you that the best way to get the max offer on your property is to create competition and have multiple offers.

### Key Thoughts

- There are various ways at your fingertips to get multiple offers right now.

- You can generate competition by using strategic scheduling.

- Don't be penny wise and pound foolish when negotiating the purchase and sales contract.

- Time is of the essence.

CHAPTER 12

# EXPECT THE BEST BUT PREPARE FOR THE WORST

*The greatest glory in living lies not in never falling, but in rising every time we fall.*
*— Nelson Mandela*[44]

## What to Do When Things Don't Work Out

When is it okay to throw in the towel? When is it okay to say, "I give up"? There is no right or wrong answer to these questions. You can't have a wish and a prayer. You need to deal with facts and not hypothetical scenarios. The decision to end your attempt to keep or sell your home comes down to the circumstances of the situation.

If the foreclosure situation involves a party who is uncooperative—for example, if a couple is getting divorced and one

179

person is not willing to sell the property or liquidate, or a person on the loan or title is deceased and their estate is not probated, or heirs are fighting over what should be done with limited time on the clock—those situations often end up at the foreclosure sale, and the bank has to just go through the normal process.

There are rare times when you can spend all your energy, you can do everything right, but the outcome will still be foreclosure because there are things that are out of your control. In those situations, it's best to understand the realities of the situation and plan your next steps accordingly.

## Giving the House Back

There are a couple of ways you can help all parties move forward when foreclosure is inevitable. You can request a short sale or provide the lender with the deed in lieu of foreclosure.

## Deed in Lieu of Foreclosure

A deed in lieu of foreclosure is exactly what it sounds like: you deed the property back to the bank so the bank doesn't have to complete the foreclosure. To facilitate this option, you will contact your servicer and let them know that you would like to surrender the deed instead of having the lender complete the foreclosure. They may or may not accept this option, depending on the chain of title and liens on the property. If the title is clouded or has issues, the property may have to go through the foreclosure process so the lender can sell it in the future.

If the lender is open to receiving a deed in lieu of foreclosure, you should request moving assistance in exchange for providing them with the deed in lieu.

## Short Sale

A short sale is when a mortgage lender agrees to accept a mortgage payoff amount less than what is owed to facilitate the sale of the property. You don't actually hand over the keys to the bank in a short sale, but you do help them facilitate a sales transaction where they won't be responsible for having more properties in their inventory. If you recall, in Chapter 3 I told you that bankers like simple things, and houses are not simple. A short sale helps them avoid dealing with houses, and bankers like that.

If you are considering a short sale, you will want to get with a broker who specializes in short sales. The process to complete a short sale can take months and can be very complicated. Your lender will want to know the details surrounding the short sale. They will want evidence of the property condition; they will want to ensure that the property was broadly marketed and that they are not being taken advantage of. You have to remember, the lender is taking a loss, so they want to make sure it is justified.

The lender also does not have to approve a short sale. They can approve or deny short sales at their discretion. They will want to see a copy of the settlement statement, and typically, the homeowner will not be able to make any profit on the sale of the house. Also, you might be required to pay back the loan shortage amount over time. Additionally, you might have tax liability from a short sale, so you will want to consult with your accountant before implementing this strategy.

## Short Sale Benefits & Disadvantages

Benefits

- You can avoid foreclosure.

- Short sales are less harmful to your credit than foreclosure.

- Short sales give you more control.

- Short sales help the lender and reduces the accumulation of legal fees.

Disadvantages

- Short sales must be approved by your lender(s).

- The lender can seek a deficiency judgement.

- There could be tax implications.

- You will lose your home.

The short-sale process can be very stressful. We once were a lender on a property in New Jersey. The homeowner was delinquent on their first and second mortgages and had numerous liens. The property's condition was suboptimal, and there was no way that the property would sell for an amount that would pay off all the debt and liens attached to the home. The homeowner was aware of this and got a real estate broker to list the home on the open market. The home was listed for numerous months, but because of the condition, no one wanted to purchase it for the amount listed. Finally, after about six months, an owner-occupant buyer with a renovation loan wanted to purchase it. However, the price he could pay was not enough to pay off all the lenders. The seller decided to conduct a short sale. The homeowner, her real estate broker, and the closing attorney all worked together to explain the situation to the lenders and lien holders. They provided concrete information about the homeowner's financial situation, the amount of time the property was listed for sale, the property condition, and the buyers' ability to close the transaction. The first mortgage holder did not agree to the short sale because their equity was protected, and they wanted to receive their full payoff amount. However, our company, as the second mortgage holder, agreed to the short sale and reduced our loan payoff by 50%. The other lien holders on the property also reduced their lien amounts. This allowed the homeowner to sell the property and avoid foreclosure.

## What to Do After the Foreclosure Sale

If your home unfortunately went to the foreclosure sale and sold at auction, it may still not be too late to save your home. Some states have a redemption period that allows borrowers to buy back their homes after the foreclosure sale. Not all states allow this, but some states do. Chapter 3 has a list of state laws with their redemption periods. Please also check for updates on the foreclosure laws for your state, as things are always changing.

Here's what you should do after the foreclosure sale:

1. Attempt to redeem your property after the sale (if your state allows for redemption and if you still want it).

2. Request overage funds if available after the sale. This is very important. If your property sells at the foreclosure sale for more than the mortgage payoff amount, you are entitled to those funds if there are no liens superior to your position on the chain of title. You should always check what your home sold for and identify if there are overage funds available.

3. Begin preparing to move. Moving sucks, and it can be a daunting process. You will have to leave the property eventually, and it is better to leave on your own accord versus being ushered out by the sheriff.

4. Communicate with the lender or buyer. Either the property went back to the lender, or it sold to a buyer at the auction. Either way, someone is going to contact you about moving out of the house so they can get possession of the property. You should communicate with them and try to work something out. If you don't communicate, they will eventually evict you.

5. Request cash for keys or moving assistance. You can ask the new owner for financial assistance to help you move. They don't have to give it to you, but they may be open to it in exchange for your getting out of the house faster.

6. Check if you have a deficiency judgment payable to your lender.

## What Not to Do

I have seen and heard of homeowners doing very strange things out of fear and frustration. Foreclosure takes a toll on the homeowner and their family. These are things you don't want to do while in foreclosure.

1. Don't move out of the house months before the foreclosure sale if you don't have anywhere to go. There is no need to start paying rent in another location if you still own the house. You should know where you are going to move to and should have a plan, but time your transition accordingly. Use this time to live rent-free and build up your savings. You will need them.

2. Don't mess up the house. There is no need to damage the house and cause others to spend more money unnecessarily. There is no need to be vindictive.

3.  Don't forget to deactivate the utilities and transfer them out of your name when you move out. You don't want a high utility bill in your name to damage your credit.

4.  Don't try to avoid service from a sheriff or process server. They will find you eventually.

---

## Chapter Goal & Key Thoughts

---

### Chapter Goal

The goal of this chapter is to let you know that it is okay for this foreclosure situation not to work out the way you anticipated.

### Key Thoughts

- Consider a short sale or deed in lieu of foreclosure if it makes sense for your specific situation.

- Request cash for keys from the buyer or lender after the foreclosure sale.

- Don't damage the property or be vindictive.

# WHAT'S NEXT

In the real estate business, I have seen so many different things. Some make you excited and some make you terrified, but all allow you to learn and grow. Once, I purchased a two-bedroom condo at a sheriff's sale. The homeowners' association was foreclosing because of lack of payment of homeowner dues. We purchased the property and proceeded with our normal policy and procedures. We sent the door knocker to knock on the door, and we posted letters for the previous owner. After numerous weeks passed with no responses and no signs of anyone living there, I went to the property with a locksmith to open the door. All the curtains and blinds were closed, and we proceeded to make entry into the property.

As soon as the locksmith opened the front door, we knew something was wrong. A grotesque smell that I had never smelled before began to seep through the doorway. We took one step into the property, and there she was: a deceased older lady sitting in her recliner. That memory echoes in my head every time I open the door of a vacant property.

I always wonder what went wrong. I don't know which one was worse, the fact that the woman died alone, the fact that no one knew she died, the fact that no one thought enough of her to check on her, or the fact that she didn't have her affairs in order. The question of what went wrong is the same question I asked when I started this book, and it's what drove me to write this book.

I want you to learn from the mistakes of others and do what is needed to successfully navigate foreclosure. It is likely that your current situation is challenging and maybe even unbearable. I want to remind you that there is light at the end of the tunnel. This is only one round out of many. As long as you have breath in your lungs and blood flowing through your veins, you have the opportunity to change your circumstance. Everyone is rooting for your success, especially me.

I'm a very competitive person, so my family and I don't typically play card or board games. It does not end well. One day, my wife and daughters were playing the card game UNO, and it started to get intense. My youngest daughter, who was five years old, was upset because she had just gotten served with a "draw two" by her older sister. She was crying incessantly and wanted to give up. I told her that she needed to sit back down and finish the game. This was not the last round. She went on to lose that round, though, and she remained angry and upset.

However, the next round she regrouped, and her hand was loaded. It was like the deck was stacked in her favor. She had all the good cards—I'm talking wild cards, "draw fours," and "draw twos." Needless to say, my five-year-old won that round. When she said, "Uno Out," she cracked a big smile, hopped up, and started jumping, dancing, singing, and everything else. Her entire disposition changed.

The same thing will happen for you with your foreclosure process.

This round is difficult. It may be tough. But the next round will always be better. You have to stay in the game. You have to stay in the fight. In the middle of this battle, you will want to quit. You will want to give up. You will want to stop fighting. But in order to sing and dance on the other side of this foreclosure obstacle, you need to keep moving forward. You can't give up! Change your mindset from surviving to thriving.

You will be on the other side of this before you know it. Focus, implement what you have learned in this book, and chart a new path moving forward. For additional help on your journey, connect with the Foreclosure Fix Family online at www.theforeclosurefix. com, and check out *The Foreclosure Fix* podcast on all platforms.

I love you, and God bless you!

# FREE FORECLOSURE RESOURCES

Please visit www.theforeclosurefix.com for additional free resources and downloads.

# GLOSSARY

**Abandonment:** the act of intentionally and permanently giving up, surrendering, deserting, or relinquishing property.

**Acceleration Clause:** a provision in a contract or promissory note that the entire amount is due and payable immediately if a specified event occurs.

**Affidavit:** a written document in which the signer swears under oath before a notary public that the statements in the document are factual.

**Allonge:** a sheet of paper attached to a negotiable instrument for endorsements that could not fit on the original instrument.

**Appraisal:** a valuation of property by an authorized party with a designation from a regulatory body governing the jurisdiction of the appraiser.

**Appreciation:** the increase in value of an asset over time.

**Assignment of Mortgage or Deed of Trust:** documents the mortgage transfer from one party to another.

**Bankruptcy:** a federal system of statutes and courts that permits persons who are insolvent to place their financial affairs under the control of the bankruptcy court.

**Cloud on Title:** an actual or apparent outstanding claim on the title to real property.

**Chain of Title:** the succession of title ownership to real property from the present owner back to the original owner at some distant time.

**Chattel:** tangible personal property that can be moved around.

**Contingency Clause:** a clause allowing one party to cancel a contract if specific requirements are unmet.

**Collateral:** an asset of value that a borrower offers as a guarantee for a loan.

**Cry:** to proclaim publicly and utter loudly.

**Due Diligence:** a process or effort to collect and analyze information before deciding or conducting a transaction so a party is not held legally liable for any loss or damage.

**Deed:** a written document that transfers ownership interest in real property to another party.

**Deed in Lieu of Foreclosure:** a deed from a homeowner conveying title of the mortgaged property to the lender as payment of the outstanding debt.

**Deed of Trust:** a document that pledges real property to secure a loan.

**Delinquency:** the state of being past due on a debt.

**Demand Letter:** a formal document sent by a lender to a borrower requesting payment to settle a delinquent mortgage.

**Default:** failure to respond to a summons and complaint served on a party in the time required by law.

**Deficiency Judgment:** a monetary judgment for an amount not covered by home securing a loan.

**Escrow:** an account held by an escrow agent into which funds are deposited for real estate transactions or the payment of taxes and insurance not yet due.

**Federal Housing Administration (FHA):** part of the U.S. Department of Housing and Urban Development. They provide mortgage insurance on loans made by FHA-approved lenders. They insure mortgages on single family homes, multifamily properties, residential care facilities, and hospitals throughout the United States and its territories.

**Forbearance:** a period of refraining from enforcing a debt that is due.

**Forced Placed Insurance:** an insurance policy purchased by a lender on a home when the property owners' insurance policy is canceled, insufficient or can't be verified.

**Interest Rate:** the price a lender charges a borrower, expressed as an annual percentage of the outstanding loan amount.

**Investor:** a person who invests their resources to earn a financial return.

**Judicial Foreclosure:** foreclosure proceedings that utilize the court system.

**Latches:** a legal claim will not be enforced if a lack of diligence or a long delay in asserting the claim hurts the opponent.

**Lien:** any official claim or charge against property or funds to pay a debt or an amount owed for services rendered.

**Lis Pendens:** Latin for "a suit pending," a written notice that a lawsuit has been filed that concerns the title to real property or some interest in that real property.

**Loss Mitigation:** the process where borrowers and their loan servicer work together to avoid a foreclosure.

**Lender:** a person or entity who lends money to make a profit.

**Loan Servicing:** the administrative aspects of a loan from when the proceeds are dispersed to the borrower until the loan is paid off.

**Maturity Date:** the date a debt matures, becomes due, and must be paid in full.

**Mortgage:** a document in which the homeowner pledges their title to real property to a lender as security for a loan described in a promissory note.

**Mortgage Statement:** a document provided by a loan servicer that outlines the important details of a loan.

**Nonjudicial Foreclosure:** the lender can foreclose on your home without filing suit or appearing in court before a judge.

**Notice of Default:** a notice to a borrower with property as security under a mortgage or deed of trust is delinquent in payments.

**Notice of Sale:** an ad or notice placed in the official newspaper for a county that includes the date, time, place, and property details for a scheduled foreclosure sale.

**Promissory Note:** a written statement of debt or promise to repay in exchange for a loan.

**Purchase and Sale Contract:** a document memorializing the mutual agreement of terms between a buyer and seller of a property.

**Payoff:** the amount owed to satisfy a loan and pay off the debt.

**Postponement:** delaying a foreclosure sale, Sheriff sale, or legal action.

**Servicer:** the party responsible for collecting mortgage payments and distributing them to the lender, tax authorities and insurers.

**Short Sale:** the process of a homeowner selling their property for less than what is owed on the mortgage(s).

**Realtor:** a member of the National Association of Realtors (NAR) and may be an agent or a broker, among other professions in the real estate industry.

**Reinstatement Quote:** gives you the exact amount needed to cure the default.

**Right of Redemptions:** the process of buying back property by paying off a loan, interest, and any foreclosure costs.

**Real Estate Agent:** a licensed professional paid a commission to help people buy and sell real estate. Real estate agents work under a real estate broker.

**Real Estate Broker:** a professional dedicated to the business of buying, selling, and renting real estate. A real estate broker is licensed to work independently and may employ real estate agents.

**Title Examination:** the real estate record search process that attempts to identify legal interests in a parcel.

**Trustee:** a person or entity who holds the assets of a trustee for the benefit of the beneficiaries.

**Trustee Sale:** a mortgage foreclosure sale initiated by the lender when a borrower defaults on their mortgage.

**Truth in Lending Act:** a federal statute that requires a commercial lender to give a borrower exact information on interest rates and a three-day period in which the borrower may compare and consider competitive terms and cancel the loan agreement.

**Unpaid Principal Balance:** the amount of a loan's principal balance that is not paid back to a lender at a specific point in time.

**Writ:** a judge's written order requiring specific action by the person or entity to whom the writ is directed.

# ACKNOWLEDGMENTS

Writing a book is a daunting task. Throughout this process, I have experienced every emotion: feelings of doubt and inadequacy, feelings of joy and enthusiasm, writer's block, fear of judgment, and grandiose plans for the future.

I did not want to write this book. I was content with helping one homeowner at a time as I worked daily in the profession I love. However, I kept coming back to this idea of wanting to impact people on a grander scale. I felt compelled to encapsulate my experiences and expertise for the layperson facing foreclosure. This book is the culmination of tens of thousands of hours of practice; thousands of conversations with homeowners, servicers, and attorneys; hundreds of meetings with property sellers; and many late nights and encouraging words from my wife, Shayna.

I want to thank God for giving me the opportunity to impact the lives of people I will never know. Special thanks to Dr. Calvin King Jr. for helping me get started in real estate and for sharing his resources when we were inexperienced and still trying to figure out if real estate was going to be a hobby or our life's mission. Thanks to Dr. Nikki Blacksmith for her feedback and research advice. Thanks to the entire Book Launchers team for your support, guidance, and professionalism.

# ABOUT THE AUTHOR

Ayodeji "DJ" Olojo is an experienced real estate investor, podcast host, and Managing Director of ASO Custom Homes, LLC. With more than 15 years of real estate investing under his belt, he's become a go-to expert on the ins and outs of foreclosure. He possesses a unique ability to analyze market trends, identify potential investment opportunities, and provide tailored solutions to homeowners facing financial hardships. DJ has a mission to help one million homeowners successfully navigate foreclosure.

Within the real estate industry, DJ has operated as a licensed builder, Realtor, landlord, debt investor, and asset manager, conducting hundreds of real estate transactions. His experience on all sides of the real estate investment process gives him unparalleled insight into what all parties may be looking for when it comes to foreclosure. His podcast, The Foreclosure Fix, gives homeowners practical advice, actionable tips, and a comprehensive understanding of the foreclosure landscape with an eye on finding hope in adversity and regaining financial footing.

DJ earned his bachelor's degree in supply chain management from Tennessee State University and later earned a master's in business administration and executive leadership from the

University of Nebraska. Away from the hustle of real estate, DJ's life revolves around his family in Metro Atlanta, GA. He is a husband and father to two girls, and when he's not working on real estate deals, he spends his time cooking, taking trips, and collecting bowties.

# ENDNOTES

1    Address, attorney name, and bid amount are fictional.

2    "Value of Mortgage Debt Outstanding in the United States from 2001 to 2022," Statista, March 2023, https://www.statista.com/statistics/274636/combined-sum-of-all-holders-of-mortgage-debt-outstanding-in-the-us/.

3    Jan Nowacki et al., "Decision Making in Response to Physiological and Combined Physiological and Psychosocial Stress," *Behavioral Neuroscience* 133, no. 1 (2019): 59–67, https://doi.org/10.1037/bne0000288.

4    "Introduction to U.S. Economy: Housing Market," Congressional Research Service, updated January 3, 2023, https://sgp.fas.org/crs/misc/IF11327.pdf.

5    Alexandria White, "73% of Americans Rank Their Finances as the No. 1 Stress in Life, According to New Capital One CreditWise Survey," CNBC, updated December 29, 2022, https://www.cnbc.com/select/73-percent-of-americans-rank-finances-as-the-number-one-stress-in-life/.

6  "State of the Global Workplace 2023 Report," Gallup, June 13, 2023, https://www.gallup.com/workplace/506879/state-global-workplace-2023-report.aspx.

7  Phil Hall, "Foreclosure Activity up 22% Year-over-Year," Weekly Real Estate News, April 19, 2023, https://wrenews.com/foreclosure-activity-up-22-year-over-year/.

8  "U.S. Foreclosure Activity Doubles Annually But Still Below Pre-Pandemic Levels," ATTOM, January 12, 2023, https://www.attomdata.com/news/market-trends/foreclosures/attom-year-end-2022-u-s-foreclosure-market-report/.

9  "Annual Number of Non-Business Bankruptcy Cases Filed in the United States from 2000 to 2022," Statista, January 2023, https://www.statista.com/statistics/817911/number-of-non-business-bankruptcies-in-the-united-states/.

10  Jessica Dickler, "Share of Americans Living Paycheck to Paycheck Rises to 63%—Here's How to Get Your Finances Back on Track," CNBC, December 15, 2022, https://www.cnbc.com/2022/12/15/amid-high-inflation-63percent-of-americans-are-living-paycheck-to-paycheck.html.

11  Abdulaziz Alhenaidi and Tim Huijts, "The Adverse Effects of Foreclosure on Mental Health in the United States after the Great Recession: A Literature Review," *Journal of Housing and the Built Environment* 35, no. 1 (2020): 335–352, https://doi.org/10.1007/s10901-019-09683-x.

12  "Stress Management," Mayo Clinic, February 3, 2022, https://www.mayoclinic.org/healthy-lifestyle/stress-management/in-depth/positive-thinking/art-20043950.

13   Emily Anderson, "Say It Loud: 5 Benefits of Reading Aloud in Your Classroom," Carnegie Learning, January 31, 2022, https://www.carnegielearning.com/blog/5-benefits-reading-aloud/.

14   Ruth Chu-Lien Chao, "Managing Stress and Maintaining Well-Being: Social Support, Problem-Focused Coping, and Avoidant Coping," *Journal of Counseling & Development* 89, no. 3 (Summer 2011): 338–348, https://doi.org/10.1002/j.1556-6678.2011.tb00098.x..

15   George Sand, *Indiana* (United States: Jefferson Press, 1902), 145.

16   Janelle Downing, "The Health Effects of the Foreclosure Crisis and Unaffordable Housing: A Systematic Review and Explanation of Evidence," *Social Science & Medicine* 162 (August 2016): 88–96, https://doi.org/10.1016/j.socscimed.2016.06.014.

17   Lauren Nowacki, "The Average Mortgage Length in The U.S.," Rocket Mortgage, June 7, 2023, https://www.rocketmortgage.com/learn/average-mortgage-length.

18   "Foreclosure," *Merriam-Webster*, accessed July 10, 2023, https://www.merriam-webster.com/dictionary/foreclosure.

19   "Everything Lenders Need to Know About Commercial Real Estate Nonjudicial Foreclosures, Total Lender Solutions," Total Lender Solutions, August 24, 2022, https://totallendersolutions.com/ultimate-lenders-guide-cre-nonjudicial-foreclosures/.

20   https://www.foreclosure.com/foreclosure_laws.html

21   "Merchandise Returned as a Percentage of Total Retail Sales in the United States from 2012 to 2022," Statista, December 2022, https://www.statista.com/statistics/876378/retail-industry-reverse-logistics-share-united-states/.

22  "U.S. Foreclosure Activity Continues to Climb in Q1 2023," ATTOM, April 19, 2023, https://www.attomdata.com/news/market-trends/foreclosures/attom-q1-2023-u-s-foreclosure-market-report/.

23  Blake Hansen, "Money Is an Amplifier," Blake Hansen, December 9, 2020, https://blakehansen.com/money-is-an-amplifier/.

24  Lorie Konish, "67% of Americans Have No Estate Plan, Survey Finds. Here's How to Get Started on One," CNBC, April 11, 2022, https://www.cnbc.com/2022/04/11/67percent-of-americans-have-no-estate-plan-heres-how-to-get-started-on-one.html.

25  Dr. DaShanne Stokes (@DaShanneStokes) "Why Trump keeps bragging about his 'genius,' 'stability,' 'greatness,' and 'hard work': - His base is shrinking - More Americans oppose him now than when he lost the popular vote - He thinks his followers are stupid - Facts are threatening to those invested in fraud," Twitter, February 11, 2019, 8:30 p.m., https://twitter.com/DaShanneStokes/status/1095132909260980226.

26  "New Data Shows FTC Received 2.8 Million Fraud Reports from Consumers in 2021," Federal Trade Commission, February 22, 2022, https://www.ftc.gov/news-events/news/press-releases/2022/02/new-data-shows-ftc-received-28-million-fraud-reports-consumers-2021-0.

27  "2023 Credit Card Fraud Report," Security.org, January 31, 2023, https://www.security.org/digital-safety/credit-card-fraud-report/.

28  "Google Local SEO Statistics That Every Search Marketer Should Read," SEO Expert, accessed July 10, 2023, https://seoexpertbrad.com/local-seo-stats/.

29  Zig Ziglar, *Better Than Good: Creating a Life You Can't Wait to Live* (New York: Thomas Nelson, 2007), 196.

30   "Buridan's Ass," Oxford Reference, accessed July 10, 2023, https://www.oxfordreference.com/display/10.1093/oi/authority.20110803095536403;jsessionid=8437C0E4F63F3A2C95F3C-C397F7EE597.

31   Tracy M. Turner and Heather Luea, "Homeownership, Wealth Accumulation and Income Status," *Journal of Housing Economics* 18, no. 2 (June 2009): 104–114, https://doi.org/10.1016/j.jhe.2009.04.005.

32   "Wealth Gains by Income and Racial/Ethnic Group," National Association of Realtors, April 19, 2023, https://www.nar.realtor/research-and-statistics/research-reports/wealth-gains-by-income-and-racial-ethnic-group.

33   "Homeowner Equity Shoots Up Again Across U.S. in Second Quarter as Home Values Keep Rising," Cision PR Newswire, August 4, 2022, https://www.prnewswire.com/news-releases/homeowner-equity-shoots-up-again-across-us-in-second-quarter-as-home-values-keep-rising-301599567.html.

34   "New Mortgage Payments Now Well Above Multifamily Rents," CBRE, April 5, 2023, https://www.cbre.com/insights/briefs/new-mortgage-payments-now-well-above-multifamily-rents.

35   "Make Money in New York Real Estate," *Munsey's Magazine,* United States: Frank A. Munsey Company, 1907.

36   "Bankruptcy," Department of Revenue, accessed July 10, 2023, https://dor.georgia.gov/bankruptcy.

37   "How the HECM Program Works," U.S. Department of Housing and Urban Development, accessed July 10, 2023, https://www.hud.gov/program_offices/housing/sfh/hecm/hecmabou.

38   Troy Doucet, *27 Legal Defenses to Foreclosure: How to Beat the Bank in Any State* (Independently published), 2021.

39  Sun Tzu, *The Art of War*, trans. Lionel Giles (New York: Cosimo Classics, 2010), 11.

40  Wayne Gretzky, interview by Bob Mackenzie, *Hockey News*, 1983.

41  Kellye Guinan and Taylor Freitas, "How Do Real Estate Agent Commissions Work?" Bankrate, January 26, 2023, https://www.bankrate.com/real-estate/realtor-fees/.

42  Harvey Mackay, "The Art of Negotiating," Harvey Mackay Academy's Blog, accessed July 10, 2023, https://harveymackayacademy.com/the-art-of-negotiating/.

43  David McMillin, "Homeowner Equity Data and Statistics," Bankrate, June 22, 2023, https://www.bankrate.com/home-equity/homeowner-equity-data-and-statistics/.

44  Nelson Mandela, *Notes to the Future: Words of Wisdom* (New York: Simon and Shuster, 2012), 93.

www.ingramcontent.com/pod-product-compliance
Lightning Source LLC
Chambersburg PA
CBHW060533160726
47991CB00001B/311